Contemporary Issues in Supply Chain Management and Logistics

Contemporary Issues in Supply Chain Management and Logistics

Anthony M. Pagano and Mellissa Gyimah

BEP BUSINESS EXPERT PRESS

Contemporary Issues in Supply Chain Management and Logistics

First published in 2017 by
Business Expert Press, LLC
222 East 46th Street, New York, NY 10017
www.businessexpertpress.com

ISBN-13: 978-1-63157-361-3 (paperback)
ISBN-13: 978-1-63157-362-0 (e-book)

Business Expert Press Supply and Operations Management Collection

Collection ISSN: 2156-8189 (print)
Collection ISSN: 2156-8200 (electronic)

Cover and interior design by Exeter Premedia Services Private Ltd., Chennai, India

First edition: 2017

10 9 8 7 6 5 4 3 2 1

Printed in the United States of America.

Abstract

This book, titled "Contemporary Issues in Supply Chain Management and Logistics," is a collection of chapters on issues we face today in the world of Supply Chain Management. While there are a number of college text books related to specific areas within logistics and supply chain issues, there are very few general supply chain management "trends" books. Thus, this book consists of seven dynamic, current and informative chapters that cover a variety of cutting-edge supply chain topics. There is an untapped market to create a supply chain and logistics book to be used in college classes that uses examples in the United States. This interdisciplinary book is of use to both graduate students and professionals working in the field because of its cutting-edge approach to emerging global issues. The book contains new, original research papers written by academics from the fields of engineering, transportation, information and decision systems, marketing, and, of course, supply chain management and logistics.

Keywords

business schools, contemporary issues, cutting-edge, education, engineering, graduate students, logistics, marketing, professional, supply chain management, transportation

Contents

Acknowledgments

A big thank you to faculty members at UIC, as well as our board members of the Center for Supply Chain Management and Logistics who all contributed directly and indirectly to this book. Thank you for your hard work and dedication to our students and supply chain globally and locally. We would also like to thank Dean Michael A. Pagano of UIC, whose vision to create the "Dean's Grant" provided some of the funding for several of the chapters in this book.

Anthony M. Pagano
Mellissa Gyimah

CHAPTER 1

Introduction—About This Book

This book, titled "Contemporary Issues in Supply Chain Management and Logistics," is a collection of chapters on issues we face today in the world of supply chain management. It consists of seven dynamic, current, and informative chapters that cover a variety of cutting-edge supply chain topics. This interdisciplinary book is of use to both graduate students and professionals working in the field because of its cutting-edge approach to emerging global issues. The book contains new, original research papers written by academics from the fields of engineering, transportation, information and decision systems, marketing, and, of course, supply chain management and logistics.

While there are a number of college text books related to specific areas within logistics and supply chain issues, there are very few general supply chain management "trends" books. Of the books that exist, the majority has a European-centered international focus. There is an untapped market to create a supply chain and logistics book to be used in college classes that uses examples in the United States. Indeed, undergraduate and graduate business schools are increasing their course offerings in logistics and supply chain management, based on student demand. Supply chain managers' salaries are increasing and c-level positions are being added to many companies. To meet this demand, these new courses will require updated and relevant books that provide timely perspectives and examples using "real-world" situations. Additionally, professionals working in the field need to stay current on the trends and issues facing supply chain managers. They will be leading their corporations' strategies on supply chain management. This book, therefore, feeds their position as thought leaders looking to make their supply chain leaner, more visionary, and reflective of the trends in supply chain management.

Chapter 2 of this book discusses research undertaken at the University of Illinois at Chicago (UIC) Center for Supply Chain Management and Logistics by UIC Professors Matt Liotine, Anthony M. Pagano, and Sidd Varma Gadiraju from Capgemini. It involves a two-year study that analyzes recent technological trends in the Logistics and Supply Chain Management space in the United States. The research focuses first on the vendors/suppliers of the technologies, progressing then to the buyers/users of these technologies. From this research, the chapter identifies emerging technologies, their implications, and acceptance, and utilization levels across various industry sectors.

Chapter 3 by William Stillman of GainSystems details the effort in trying to minimize the negative financial impacts of "Murphy's Law." This issue has challenged the executive suite for years. Corporations have spent hundreds of millions of dollars on outside consulting firms and enterprise software trying to manage the impact of "Murphy" on their inventory investment and operating costs. It then discusses a method to consistently achieve the "Perfect Order." To achieve this with the maximum contribution to margin, one needs to plan across the enterprise at the most granular level. Therefore, one needs to account in that plan for all variables and needed to monitor the enterprise to identify any changes in Stock Keeping Unit Location (SKUL) behavior patterns, customer behavior patterns, or other relevant elements of the enterprise supply chain.

Fazle Karim and Professor Houshang Darabi of UIC review, in Chapter 4, the methods for demand forecasting and provide a comprehensive framework for the prediction of the demand of location-dependent services such as healthcare facilities, retail stores, banks, restaurants, and so on. The chapter discusses how accurate forecasting is becoming vital for survival and success of business, and how demand forecasting is also becoming the foundation of location-dependent services as it helps with marketing and revenue.

Chapter 5, written by Mellissa Gyimah, explores and discusses how education and academic intersect within supply chain management, and what people in the workforce look for as an educational foundation for students they would potentially hire. Essentially, what coursework do companies appreciate and value most so that potential employees are effective in their company as workers? Using a survey method and analyzing individual's responses, we see the skills and educational background companies prefer and how it would be beneficial for companies and universities to collaborate moving forward.

The team of Pourabdollahi, Karimi, Mohammadian, and Kawamura are the authors of Chapter 6. This chapter is based on the PhD thesis of Zahra Pourabdollahi, now at RS&H, Inc in Tampa. Behzad Karimi of the University of South Florida, Professors Kouros Mohammadian and Kazuya Kawamura of UIC round out the team. In Chapter 6, we are exposed to the remarkable increase in freight movements and their significant impacts on the transportation system, regional well-being, and economic growth. This provides sufficient motivation to develop reliable analysis tools to estimate commodity flows between zones and forecast the future demand and trends of goods movements among regions. The chapter illustrates the need to develop freight demand models to better facilitate infrastructure planning and policy development by outlining a behavioral agent-based supply chain and freight transportation model for the Chicago Metropolitan Area. This multimodal freight model addresses critical technical and conceptual hurdles that have challenged past efforts by applying an agent-based framework.

The initial part of Chapter 7, written by Professor Chis Westland of UIC, addresses the research question of how you create an accurate customer demand forecast for a single item inventory where demand is indirectly observed by tracking inventory levels. Inventory management and control are often myopic. The only information that management has available for the customer demand input to their policy model comes from the inventory levels over time, which is inherently right-censored by stockouts (where demand exceeds supply). The remainder of the chapter delineates a methodology to address customer demand forecast errors that can contribute to suboptimization in supply-chain algorithms. It introduces a separable demand forecasting based on Kaplan–Meier estimators using data only from inventory levels, while providing examples of the application of such estimators to elicit demand forecast time-series. Finally, the chapter incorporates the forecasts generated from Kaplan–Meier estimators using data only from inventory levels into a basic inventory restocking algorithm.

Chapter 8, written by Anthony M. Pagano, discusses Public–Private Partnerships (PPP) that is in the forefront of approaches to funding transportation infrastructure improvements. Highlighted in the highway area by long-term leases of the Chicago Skyway and Indiana Toll Road, a variety of states are investigating the use of PPP either as "Brownfield" leases such as the Chicago and Indiana cases, or "Greenfield" Design, Build, Operate, Transfer arrangements. These and other PPP projects raise a variety of issues, including the length of the lease, toll escalation permitted, and use of funds. This paper develops a rationale for PPPs in transportation, evaluates several approaches to PPPs using this rationale, and analyzes some of the difficult issues that can surface.

CHAPTER 2

Technology Trends in Logistics and Supply Chain Management

Matthew Liotine, Anthony M. Pagano, and Siddhartha Varma Gadiraju

Overview of Research

This research, undertaken by the University of Illinois at Chicago's Center for Supply Chain Management and Logistics, involves a two-year study, which works toward analyzing the recent technological trends in the Logistics and Supply Chain Management space in the United States, which are being followed by major corporations. The research focuses first on the vendors/suppliers of the technologies discovered, progressing then to the buyers/users of these technologies.

Objectives

- Identify the emerging technologies, either hardware or software, that companies are investing in, currently, and in the short term.
- Understand the implications of the technologies with respect to areas that include value creation, operational effectiveness, investment level, technical migration, and general industry acceptance.
- Identify short-term trends in the technology acceptance and utilization levels across various industry sectors.
- Characterize the supply chain and logistics applications in which the technologies are being utilized with regard to

product planning, materials management and inventory,
transportation, distribution, workflow, plant maintenance,
quality assurance, environment, health, and safety.
- Identify favored suppliers for the technologies identified.

Study Approach

The team has interviewed a group of 10 companies that provide various
innovative technological services for industry giants in North America
and elsewhere. The choice of vendors was made based on the innovative
quality of their product/service, its usability, and adaptability in regard
to current supply chain practices and associated return on investment
(ROI).

A list of companies has been included in the following table, along
with their associated field of service in the supply chain space. While there
is much diversity in the services and products provided by these companies, they all contribute to optimizing complex, global supply chains.
A comprehensive view of how these different technologies interact with
each other to have a positive impact on the supply chain operations is
provided in this report.

To get a better idea of the desired functionality of new supply chain
technologies in the industry, an interview with the Aberdeen Group was
also conducted. Aberdeen, as a company with a supply chain research
unit, has been able to shed some light on the recent trends in the supply
chain industry.

Study Findings

Overview

Overall, companies have been integrating new technologies in their supply chain and logistics operations for numerous reasons. Among these are:

- To improve ROI by using technologies that better leverage
  utilization of capital expenditures in people and equipment.
- To create operational efficiencies in order to reduce inventory
  and improve cycle times.

- To improve customer responsiveness by reducing lead times, improving product availability, and offering flexibility to changing customer demands.

All of these ultimately result in creating greater value for the customer base, and consequently improved profitability. To this end, companies are seeking ways to establish greater end-to-end visibility across the complexity of supply chain and logistics operations, processes, and systems. Visibility provides "controlled access and transparency to accurate, timely and complete events and data (transactions, content and relevant supply chain information) within and across organizations and to support effective planning and execution of supply chain operations" [1].

Table 2.1 illustrates these relationships as they existed at the outset of this study. Until recently, technology has been considered as an enabler for improvements in underlying supply chain and logistics operations. However, recent trends in society and business such as mobile computing,

Table 2.1 List of Companies

Company name	Services	Website
SAP	Enterprise Resource Planning	www.sap.com/index.html
Vuzix	Hardware—for Optimized Warehouse Operations	www.vuzix.com/
ORTEC	Software Solutions—Advanced Planning and Optimization	http://ortec.com/
Aberdeen Group	Industry Research	www.aberdeen.com/
Accenture	Management Consulting and Technology Services	www.accenture.com/
Mecalux	Industrial, Racking, and Storage Solutions	www.interlakemecalux.com/
GT Nexus	Cloud-based Supply Chain Services	www.gtnexus.com/
Bastian Solutions	Material Handling Systems Integrator	www.bastiansolutions.com/
AGV Solutions	Automated Guided Vehicle Systems Provider	http://agvsolutions.com/
Zebra Technologies	Tracking Technology and Solutions	www.zebra.com

Figure 2.1 Supply chain and logistics relationships

social media, and online retailing have significantly changed almost every aspect of the supply chain and logistics landscape. In this study, the following technologies were found to have a pervasive role in altering this landscape (Figure 2.1):

- *Maturing technologies*
  Based on industry study, the following technologies are considered maturing technologies, whose aim is to improve service and efficiency.
  - o Optimization software
  - o Sensors/telematics
  - o Cloud computing
  - o Data warehouse and integration
  - o Automated storage and retrieval

  Current adoption levels for these technologies are at 35 percent and are projected to reach 80–90 percent by 2019 [2].
- *Growth technologies*
  The following technologies are considered growth technologies, whose adoption rates are currently about 20 percent, but are expected to grow steadily in the next three to five years [2].
  - o Mobility
  - o Wearability
  - o Data analytics
  - o Social media

- *Emerging technologies*

  The following technologies are considered emerging technologies, with current adoption rates of 10 percent [2]. These technologies are viewed as disruptive in nature, and thus have the potential to significantly alter supply chain and logistics operations in unforeseen ways:

  o 3D printing

  o Drones

  o Autonomous vehicles

Specific Findings

It is important to note that the impacts of these technologies in many cases are collective rather than individual, the result of integrating a technology with one or more of the others. The following briefly describe their impacts as identified in this study:

Cloud Computing

Cloud computing technology has enabled companies to migrate platforms and applications that were once predominantly on-premises or within public/private cloud environments. Cloud computing is a technology that provides user applications that are delivered from a collected group of distributed computing resources (e.g., servers, databases, applications, networks, etc.). Cloud computer offerings have been classified into Software as a Service (SaaS), Platform as a Service (PaaS), and Infrastructure as a Service (IaaS). SaaS consumers use a provider's applications running on a cloud infrastructure, accessing them using various client devices through a thin client interface such as a Web browser. The underlying cloud infrastructure includes network, servers, operating systems, and storage that are invisible to the customer. SaaS providers are likely to be PaaS consumers, paying for memory, storage environments, and tools when they create SaaS applications. PaaS providers are consumers of IaaS providers, who offer cloud resources as virtualized resource pools, again masking the underlying computing and communications infrastructure that comprise the cloud.

The benefits of cloud computing include lower implementation costs, faster time to value, and cost-effective upgrades, among others. The capital savings that cloud computing offers has made rapid deployment of ubiquitous information sharing solutions more cost-effective. The use of private clouds has enabled the orchestration of capacity sharing and management across the various players in a supply chain. Clouds can be multienterprise in nature, and thus provide a group of supply chain partners at different tiers with controlled, real-time access and transparency to data events. Clouds provide the ability for multiple enterprises to access and share information such as inventory, capacity, and logistics data. Transportation management systems (TMS) have been cloud-oriented for some time, but warehouse management systems have been slow to move to the cloud, due to insufficient response times when connecting to terminal and material handling systems. However, it is envisioned that this trend will change with technology improvements.

As an example, GT Nexus provides a solution for making use of the vast amounts of data that are collected in a supply chain, often using big data approaches. They offer a cloud-based platform for companies in a supply chain to share logistics data in real time. The cloud platform serves as data hub in which companies are brought to the data and not the other way around. This provides full visibility of updated data across the supply chain.

For instance, status information regarding orders and shipments is maintained on the cloud, so that it can be used to monitor the flow across suppliers or logistic service providers or both, and to circulate alert notifications if any disruption occurs. Over time, notifications can collectively be used to help brand certain suppliers or service providers, thus enabling firms to better manage risks.

Another example of the use of clouds in supply chains is in regard to collaborative sourcing, which is multiple bidding over one central cloud platform [3]. Implemented as a SaaS approach, this approach is envisioned to gradually replace older, traditional sourcing methods. Cloud-based collaborative sourcing can save organizations an average of 20.7 percent [4]. The GT Nexus network can track supplier and buyer history, and credit strength, which can be used to better assess risk.

Mobility

Mobility has spawned greater variability in customer demand patterns that have greatly influenced warehouse and delivery operations. Additionally, mobility has also offered the ability to influence customer buying through customer location awareness using GPS. For example, by establishing presence zones in retail stores via Wi-Fi, retailers can offer promotions to a customer's mobile device based on their location.

Mobile technology provides a number of additional capabilities for supply chain and logistics at a much lower cost than traditional technologies. These include capabilities such as bar-code scanning, document management, GPS tracking, real-time field work force management, shipment tracking, and real-time proof of delivery. Many of these technologies can now be implemented using widely available smartphones and tablets.

In addition, the data derived from mobile devices and connected businesses provides a feed for predictive analytics. For example, equipment and vehicle breakdowns can be anticipated, or a series of events that needs further investigation can be flagged. This enables organizations to convert unplanned, expensive maintenance into planned downtime, thereby improving efficiency and cost-effectiveness [5].

Companies have recently started to adopt enterprise mobility solutions for improved supply chain visibility and traceability. With real-time information available to key supply chain personnel, better and more accurate decision making is made possible. For example, identifying the problem points in a supply chain, and consequently arriving at an informed solution, becomes easier. To meet this demand, enterprise mobility platforms have sprung up, with mobile technology becoming increasingly cheaper.

Wearability

Wearable technology moves applications and apps away from mobile phones and devices to enable hands-free voice and gesture-driven movements in warehouse and field service operations. A conversation with SAP revealed such trends as they are being used in warehouses. One such trend is the use of smart glasses for enhanced workflow, specifically the M100, designed by Vuzix used for effective warehouse operations. Augmented reality applications designed for the smart glass environment will help in better coordination between employees to cut down on task completion time and other benefits.

Wearable technology such as smart glasses can enhance worker accuracy, reduce mistakes, and improve safety for front-line workers. Adoption levels for both mobile and wearable technology are currently at 23 percent and are expected to reach 64 percent in the next 3 to 5 years [2].

There is an increased demand for migrating from smartphone and tablet-based augmented reality applications to wearable devices. Companies such as BMW, Audi, Boeing, and Airbus are trying to achieve this for their designed applications. Vuzix makes this possible through their SmartGlass products, especially the M100. The M100 SmartGlass provides an enhanced workflow especially in the industrial, medical, and retail sectors by providing a hands-free experience and also enhancing capability. The M100 is an Android-based device.

The M100 has three modes of operation:

1. The normal mode of operation where the android applications run on the M100 processor. Play Store applications designed for Android-based smartphones and tablets will run on the device without a problem. But further optimization is required for it to be seamlessly integrated into the SmartGlass environment.
2. The laptop display operation where the device connects to laptops or personal computers and shows the display of the connected device instead.
3. Handshaking with other devices for real-time information transfer.

The battery life of the M100 had to be traded off for size since the device has to be very light, for prolonged usage. But there is an option of an additional battery that increases the expected battery life. With the current specifications, the device is expected to run for around eight hours of usage without video streaming or power draining AR (augmented reality) applications. With video streaming and applications, this comes down to around two hours of heavy usage. But with the additional battery, this can be extended to two days.

The device has to undergo Specific Absorption Rate (SAR) and Federal Communication Commission (FCC) testing and other regulatory exercises. There are other obstacles that have to be tackled such as the wearability issues that have to be addressed in the case of people with prescription lenses. Security is another major concern as information is quite easy to access though the glasses.

Customers of Vuzix (usually enterprises), in general, either write their own code (for customized applications) or work with companies that partner with Vuzix to provide for this demand. Middleware and front-end development are very expensive, especially when the need for customization must be taken into account. Vuzix is partnering with SAP for this purpose. SAP has taken up the middleware and front-end development requirement. They have recently announced two AR applications that help simplify and improve the user experience and work processes by offering a hands-free working experience: SAP AR Warehouse Picker and SAP AR Service Technician applications. These applications that boast doubled efficiency, hence allowing warehouse picking to be done twice as fast as current methods, are in demand with companies such as DHL, FedEx, Pepsi, Coke, and Walmart.

The selling point of the M100 is that it is responsive to voice and gesture instead of the standard keyboard-based entry. This allows for a hands-free experience that is quite preferred in warehouse environments. But Android applications still need to be optimized to make better usage of these devices' capabilities. Vuzix is willing to provide the APIs for development of such applications to the customers. Another advantage is that the device will save money ultimately since it replaces technology in current usage, such as barcode scanners, with powerful video and image-processing functionalities. Migration is hence not a huge issue, since Vuzix is willing to provide for software customization in an advisory capacity. Vuzix also provides a very user-friendly interface. This is helpful for the workers who need to adopt an entirely new system of operation. Since the user interface is intuitive, employees do not need an extensive training period for this transition. The M100 provides 10–15 voice commands by default, but additional libraries can be used if required.

Another approach is voice. KPM, which is a distributor of outdoor power equipment in the Northeast United States, relies on Lydia Plug and Play voice solutions from topVox. The worker wears a headset to hear directions and respond back [6].

Data Analytics

Data analytics involves the manipulation and computation of large volumes of data, often from a wide variety of different sources. Manipulation and computation is performed at high velocity to identify patterns, correlations, and other useful information. Data analytics capabilities have been found to enhance the utility of the mass amounts of data that can be collected and communicated through the supply chain on a regular basis. Not only can information be distilled more quickly, but models can be developed to aid decision making at all levels of the supply chain. Examples include:

- Understanding buyer/supplier behavior to reduce inventory levels.
- Using predictive analytics to predict maintenance events in equipment so that parts and labor resources can be effectively prepositioned for repairs.
- Using analytics to support real-time dynamic decision making as to how to pick and ship orders based on current situational awareness of demand patterns.
- Creating online promotions hourly, based on buying demand to reduce inventory levels.

The current adoption level for predictive analytics is 25 percent and is expected to reach 70 percent in 3 to 5 years, and up to 77 percent in 6 years [2]. The strategic use of data analytics has been to provide up-to-date information to make decisions and respond appropriately. Doing so can enhance agility to respond to uncertain market conditions. This feature can help reduce risk, especially in emerging markets where volatile conditions can complicate growth and production [7].

In the transportation sector, there has been a shift from using traditional transportation management systems to their integration with decision-making analytics tools, so as to not just record but analyze transportation data and make suggestions accordingly. Predictive analytics can provide critical predictions for field service, and can be used to strategically position parts and personnel before problems or issues arise. This not only reduces parts inventory, but ensures overall service quality and reliability [8].

For example, Accenture was approached for its multinational presence, and its consequent knowledge of global trade and trends. Accenture has recently collaborated with General Electric on a predictive analytics project (TALERIS) to provide an intelligent operations service for airline carriers around the globe. Another example is health products retailer GNC who uses a labor management dashboard in distribution centers to track picking completion times and variances, enabling them to shift resources accordingly to keep up with demand. Using data analytics for supply chain management can also optimize shipping. For example, United Parcel Service (UPS) has been working for a decade on a system called On-Road Integrated Optimization and Navigation (ORION) that determines the optimal path for road delivery, using big data analytics to handle the data encountered [9, 10].

SAP has recently produced a High-Performance Analytic Appliance (HANA) platform, which is effectively "live cache" technology. HANA can be used to support an in-memory relational database management system (RDBMS). This technology can dramatically increase the run-time speed of various complex applications in the supply chain, and can transform what were once operational tools into decision-making tools. Speed is achieved by virtue of in-core processing and avoiding the need for data aggregation. For example, a materials requirements plan (MRP), which traditionally took hours to run, can now produce results in seconds. Such speed can enable companies to run multiple MRPs to achieve the most desirable scenarios. Another example is in warehouse management, where it is used to track warehouse employees in real time by managing data that tracks historic movements of employees. Such information can be used to predict task completion times, making labor management more efficient.

Data Warehouse and Integration

The amount of data being generated on a daily basis is staggering, and using standard data analytic tools for pulling meaningful data from these enormous data sets is not a practical task. As automation in the supply chain grows, so does the volume of real-time or near real-time transactional data that is generated from automated systems. This data must be used in conjunction with master (or fixed) data for process execution and monitoring. Big data analytics works mainly with transactional data to provide real-time analytic information that complements the end-to-end visibilities of a supply chain.

Faster and cheaper computer power has accelerated the use of big data warehouse solutions in the supply chain and logistics arena. The drivers for cost-effective data warehousing have been the push for the use of big data and both real-time and predictive analytics. Consequently, data warehouse technologies underpin many of the capabilities offered by the other technologies described in this study. Many of these technologies are attributed to hardware innovations such as high-capacity Random Access Memory (RAM), multicore processor architectures, massive parallel scaling and processing, and large symmetric multiprocessors.

Such innovations have led to the use of an architected data warehouse with in-memory technology as a preferred approach [11]. An architected approach is more cost-effective versus a loosely architected system of components. In-memory technology reduces data processing time, improves flexibility and scalability, and reduces the need for data transformation and aggregation. On the other hand, the use of in-memory databases can encounter performance problems when transferring large volumes of data from memory to cache. Thus, there needs to be good compatibility between the data warehouse platform and the data analytics software that is performing the querying.

The use of data virtualization with this approach can further reduce the data design effort, data movement, data redundancy, and ultimately costs. It also eliminates integration issues across varying types of data sets. On the other hand, it requires careful system performance management such that response times are not degraded in light of varying kinds of data queries. Virtualization can also help data warehouses with accommodating unstructured data forms such as documents, videos, and images. Such varied formats of data can potentially clutter the data warehouse unnecessarily, and require new interfaces on the part of the data warehouse to input and output such data.

Sensors and Telematics

Remote operation and control (ROC) has become more popular in supply chain and logistics in order to achieve greater operational visibility. Control center types of operations, while traditionally popular in industries such as pipelines and railroads, have now found their place in other industries, such as retail. Sensor technologies such as Radio Frequency Identification (RFID) and telematics have been recognized recently for their potential in the supply chain area and have capabilities to provide the ability to extend the reach of this control beyond a firm's own supply chain. For example, capabilities such as end-to-end monitoring of shipments and containers, and event management and alerting, can help control the bullwhip effect. Zebra Technologies is a major player in the RFID scene, and were helpful in this study in shedding light on how these technologies can have a massive impact on tackling future supply chain visibility issues.

By powering the Internet of Things (IOT), these sensors provide insight into patterns and also help with keeping track of a company's assets. For example, one can predict and optimize trip time using sensors. Predicting when shipments will be late allows logistics managers to immediately notify customers, rebook warehouse loaders, or reschedule cross-docking operations. Analyzing data over time allows managers to optimize routes and schedules to reduce travel time, plan cross-dock plans with fewer disconnects, and ascertain which drivers provide the best results by route, season, and time of day.

This solution combines data from sensor, supply chain logistics, weather, traffic, and more, and applies machine learning to detect repeatable patterns that managers can use to predict transit times and delays under a variety of circumstances. It presents this information in graphical interfaces that managers can access in seconds from any computer, tablet, or smartphone, enabling them to make decisions whenever they are most useful.

Asset utilization is also better handled using sensor technology. Maximizing freight capacity while minimizing fleet waste is another top concern. Typically, this is done by combing reports that are manually tallied and assembled across many levels of the organization, which is labor-intensive and error-prone.

On the other hand, sensors provide direct "eyes and ears" when assets are in use and when they are idle. It does this without making human time and effort to record and combine information. Combining sensor data with order information allows logistics managers to view a complete picture of asset utilization. For example, not only can managers see when their vehicles were planned for deliveries, they can also know when the vehicle left the yard, when it was actually moving and when it arrived inside the delivery location. Managers can also monitor the driving habits of individual drivers. Thus, the carrier can use the truck longer prior to leaving without affecting the next delivery time [12].

It should be noted that there is too much data. Data granularity must be decided upon by companies prior to set up, based on both storage capacity and capability of its analytic operations. In some cases, Big Data analytics must be employed to handle the data generated by a multitude of sensors, in order to capture patterns and make informed business decisions.

3D Printing

3D printing has a direct impact on the supply chain. The opportunity for on-demand manufacturing and the quick production of more customized products that 3D printing offers can reduce lead time, inventory and waste, warehouse costs, and other inefficiencies, while improving product quality. Although manufacturing in some locations can be low-cost, operating a global logistics network, including transportation and other distribution expenses, means huge overhead costs. 3D printing can help reduce these overhead costs by enabling businesses to station local manufacturing centers closer to strategic markets, hence reducing the length and complexity of a supply chain while simultaneously helping reduce the carbon footprint. Regional manufacturing centers will help with inventory concerns, specifically in terms of highly customized goods for consumers. The cost of customization will be brought down significantly, while the range and scope of customization simultaneously increase.

There has been a recent trend in ecommerce: next-day delivery. 3-D printing can make this more viable, with customers being able to expect highly specialized requests to go through in a matter of hours. With the reduction in transportation and sourcing time, retailers, either online or otherwise, will be able to deliver quality goods exceptionally fast. Moreover, the price of the product itself would go down. These advantages could be extended beyond retail, and 3D printing has found popularity in the aerospace, defense, automotive, healthcare, and consumer products industries.

The major applications of 3D printing include new product prototyping, small runs of high-value replacement parts, and complex customized products [2]. While this technology has much promise in the future, there are very few examples of its implementation today. Current adoption levels of 3D printing is about 10 percent, but is expected to change significantly within the next six years.

Social Media

Global supply chains by definition are very large and include a number of vendors, distribution centers, suppliers, buyers, manufacturing plants, logistics service providers, and so on. Social media can be used as a mechanism for collective intelligence about a supply chain by gathering information from a broad base of different sources. This collective intelligence can be used to uncover evolving trends or for better-informed decision making.

For example, identifying "social sentiment" has found its way into supply chain and logistics operations with respect to supplier sourcing. Social sentiment on potential vendors and suppliers can be used to support supplier qualification and performance monitoring. It can also be used to identify product design and lot problems. Websites such as Procurious.com has been emerging, acting as portals through which supply chain professionals can interact and build stronger relationships. CH Robinson, a leading global third-party logistics (3PL) provider, launched *TMC Connect*, a social media site specifically offered for supply chain clients to interact. Since its launching in December 2009, supply chain executives and related key personnel within their customer community have become active members [13].

Social media benefits the supply chain industry in many ways. Companies can enhance communication with customers, generate demand, reduce operating costs, mitigate risk, increase productivity, and enhance marketplace intelligence. If companies aren't participating in social media, they could be at a disadvantage because most of their customers, suppliers, and competitors are. Social media can help companies improve supply chain processes and solve existing problems by accessing the collective insights of supply chain trading partners.

Drones

Drone technology has been around for some time now, but its usage for commercial purposes is strictly regulated in America. Unmanned aircraft can cost-effectively automate what were once cost-intensive manual activities, such as field inspection in remote area or those that are difficult to access, using aircraft equipped with cameras or RFID transponders. Oil companies are also considering employment of drones for certain operations [2]. For example, if there is a pipeline malfunction, it is much easier to send a drone out to scout for the cause or location of the malfunction than sending trucks to check the situation. A firm called PINC Air uses drones to track assets in yards. The drones would be used in conjunction with traditional yard management systems [14].

Online retailers are also considering drones for cost-effective last-mile access and delivery. By 2017, 20 percent of logistics organizations are likely to exploit drones for use in their operations. For example, Amazon has been trying to add drones to their delivery service, through Prime Air, but has faced resistance from the United States Federal Aviation Administration (FAA). Amazon has recently been cleared for prototype testing, which opens up doors for several companies to introduce this technology in the future. Also, Domino's Pizza has started experiments of drone delivery of pizza.

Automated Storage and Retrieval Systems

Another trend is the increasing use of automated elements in the warehouse. An Automated Storage and Retrieval System (AS/RS) is an integration of automated equipment and controls that can handle, store, and retrieve materials as needed with high precision, accuracy, and speed. Such systems vary from simple, manually controlled order-picking machines operating in small storage structures to massively large, computer-controlled systems that are totally integrated into a manufacturing and distribution process.

Specifically, AS/RS refers to a variety of computer-controlled methods for automatically storing and retrieving loads to and from defined locations. Within an AS/RS environment one would find one or more of the following technologies: horizontal carousels, vertical carousels, vertical lift modules, and fixed aisle (F/A) storage and retrieval systems. F/A systems utilize special storage retrieval machines to perform the work needed to insert, extract, and deliver loads to designated input/output locations.

Since warehouse density tends to vary inversely with the number of different items stored, AS/RSs have been found to provide multifold improvements in warehouse productivity in today's environment where the number and diversity of Stock Keeping Units (SKUs) is rapidly growing.

The benefits of adopting an AS/RS system are quite evident. For one, they improve the organization of products in a warehouse, also allowing for more storage space due to high density storage and narrower aisles. They also reduce labor (and associated) costs, while simultaneously improving safety conditions.

Warehouse redesign is an integral part of shifting to an automated system. Mecalux is one such company that provides warehouse solutions such as design and manufacturing of steel racking and other storage solutions. Bastian Robotics is another company that provides turnkey solutions for companies, including implementations of fast pick-and-place robots for enhanced accuracy and speed. Further information about Mecalux and Bastian Solutions can be found in the appendixes.

Autonomous Vehicles

An automated guided vehicle or automatic guided vehicle (AGV) is a mobile robot, most often used in industrial applications for material handling purposes around a manufacturing facility or warehouse. There has been a steady increase in usage of AGVs in the past few decades, due to decreasing cost. AGVs are employed across multiple industries, primarily pharmaceutical, chemical, manufacturing, automotive, and warehousing. AGVs follow different navigation models; some follow markers or wires on the floor, some use vision, and so on. Selection of a model is done based on current requirement and budget. Currently, laser-based AGVs are in high demand and usage. Recent trends are seeing integration with vision systems/image sensors for a wider range of applications.

Common AGV applications include raw materials handling, work-in-process movement, pallet handling, finished product handling, trailer loading, roll handling, and container handling. As with all automated systems, usage of AGVs leads to labor reduction, improved safety, and inventory control. These benefits lead to decreased overall cost, and a two-year payback is generally anticipated. Implementation times may vary from six months to one year, based on requirement and the necessity of integration with current systems. Autonomous vehicles have been found to improve productivity for routine operations involving movement of goods and materials. These improvements include enhanced safety, energy savings, operational efficiency, and increased accuracy and consistency.

AGV Solutions was approached for this study. AGV Solutions is a provider of AGVs in the North American market. AGV Solutions offers a complete line of standard and custom AGVs. These AGVs offer payloads from a few pounds to 65 tons, lifting heights up to 36 feet with the use of many types of navigation such as laser, vision, contour, wire, magnet, and tape.

AGV Solutions' vehicles are usually integrated with the client's current warehouse management system. Full software support is provided with the control software offered. The onboard control system is developed to be less costly compared to other technologies, without compromising the functionality, flexibility, and quality required, and provides access to the AGV's sensors and other additions.

Caterpillar has also been using autonomous vehicles in mining. In addition, Google has developed and tested an autonomous vehicle for passenger use. The passenger vehicle faces many regulatory challenges and may not be in commercial use for some time.

Overall, AGVs have been found to improve productivity for routine operations involving movement of goods and materials. These improvements include enhanced safety, energy savings, operational efficiency, and increased accuracy and consistency. These vehicles have seen increased usage in material handling in manufacturing and warehouses. By 2030, AGVs are expected to represent approximately 25 percent of the passenger vehicle population in mature markets. Further information on AGV Solutions can be found in the appendixes.

Electronic Shelving

Electronic shelf labeling (ESL) is used by innovative retailers for greater operational efficiency. ESL makes possible automatic price and information labeling of items, and customer engagement in the mobility-driven customer paradigm. The ESLs are controlled using state-of-the-art wireless technology and can optimize processes such as inventory management and self-checkout.

With ESLs, price changes can be made based on consumer preferences or the inventory levels of a specific location. This enables retailers to deploy new advertising and promotional campaigns to stores in seconds or minutes instead of weeks or months. The demand for these systems is increasing, with major retail companies looking at the ESL value proposition. Major vendors of ESL systems include SES (Store Electronic Systems) and Pricer.

Compass Marketing Inc., partnering with Panasonic, has been working on Powershelf, a system that replaces the billions of paper price tags with labels that display price electronically, allowing retailers to change prices remotely in minutes. The system, expected to be incorporated with weight sensors, will also help with out-of-stock inventory costs, aid in marketing, and help with overall customer experience.

ESL systems are currently being embraced more in European nations, but the demand in America has also been high, and growing. There have been reports of a 100 percent ROI in one-and-a-half to two years, with replacement only needed every five years [15]. A conservative 5 percent implementation of ESL in the U.S. market and 20 percent implementation in European market, values the total market to reach just over € 3 billion by 2018.

Optimization Software

While optimization software has been utilized in supply chain and logistics operations for some time now, more standardized off-the-shelf packages have become available. Additionally, software packages are becoming more equipped with integration capabilities with other systems such as Enterprise Resource Planning (ERP) and warehouse management systems, as well as field and floor technologies. While traditionally such packages involved a high level of optimization capabilities, they are now featuring more data analytics capabilities. Consequently, this transforms the package into a decision-making analytics tool, and not just a mechanical optimization calculator. The popular areas of applications include inventory management (ordering, picking, sourcing, etc.), transportation management (loading, auditing, payment, etc.), and manufacturing management (contract manufacturing strategies).

Another visible trend is the integration of this software into a supply chain execution (SCE) technology platform, which represents a collection of logistics software applications, also referred to as advanced planning systems (APS). This includes warehouse management systems (WMS), transportation management systems (TMS), labor management systems (LMS), supply chain visibility, analytics, and other capabilities. As of today, very few companies have yet to implement this kind of integrated platform, relying on loosely integrated solutions from multiple vendors [16]. However, it is envisioned that many firms will be seeking single vendor suites. Many companies are looking to move from a heterogeneous collection of applications into a well-integrated software platform.

One WMS capability that is highly desired among firms is inventory control [16], followed by flow of goods management. For TMS systems, freight pay, audit, and routing are considered highly desirable. Tighter integration between these two modules would entail the passing of detailed transportation plans to the WMS for execution, with the WMS issuing exceptions back to the TMS.

Use of optimization packages can amount to potential savings in vehicle routing, load building, and logistics network design by 10 percent or more [2], with larger potential reduction in total inventory costs. Additionally, these packages can help achieve ROI in load building at 5–10% and 3–5% in network design. One company that provides this service is ORTEC, along with other services such as load building and network design solutions.

Summary

Ecommerce has created high demand variability and changed demand patterns from what was a once seasonal (or lumpy) pattern to a jagged pattern. This trend, coupled with the growth in the volume and multiplicity of SKUs and the demand for direct shipping has challenged the traditional supply chain and logistics landscape in several ways. It has created major effects on warehouse management due to the increase in direct shipping demand from the distribution center to the customer, and consequently has required traditional pick, pack, and ship operations to be more fluid. Overall, technology enablers that can support improving fulfillment are being sought, and that can tightly integrate with existing ERP systems.

One of the most important findings has been that technology, irrespective of the field it services, adapts at a tremendous pace. While it is not possible to keep track of every emerging and evolving trend in individual systems while managing other business operations, it is possible to rely on organizations that are designed for this sole purpose. Major multinational corporations have hence been outsourcing their supply chain planning and optimization needs to 3PL service providers so they can focus on other issues. This saves time and research effort for these corporations, while simultaneously improving efficiency as 3PL service providers and vendors are in possession of valuable and current domain-specific knowledge in an area as dynamic as the logistics and supply chain field. Different vendors will cater to different parts of a company's supply chain, while it is up to the firm to integrate these components into a supply chain optimization process.

Future Vision

A current view of the future technology architecture of the supply chain is portrayed in Figure 2.2. Illustrated are the roles within the supply chain of the component technologies that were studied. To a great extent, many of the component technologies that were studied are gradually being used to automate supporting facilities such as the plant, warehouse, and distribution centers, as well as transportation vehicles. Integration within

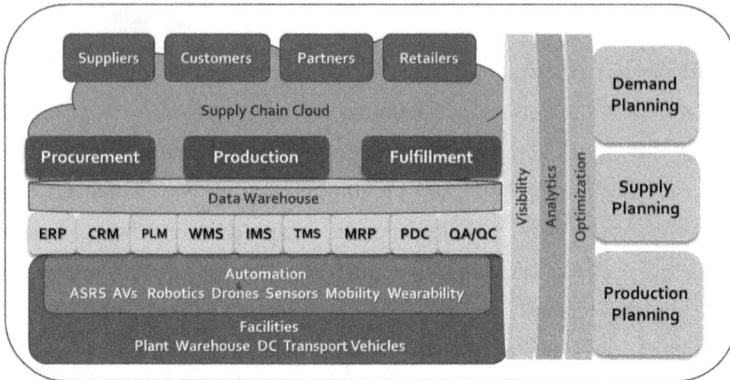

Figure 2.2 Supply chain management future vision

many of the support systems is required to enable control and monitoring. Commensurate with this integration is the collection and movement of vast amounts of data across systems, and the ability to store that data in data warehouses for widespread utilization within the firm to support procurement, production, and fulfillment operations. Cloud technology can be viewed as the backplane that enables information collection and sharing with other supply chain stakeholders such as suppliers, customers, retailers, and other partners. It also makes possible both horizontal and vertical visibility of the supply chain operations. The use of analytics and optimization tools can aid management decision-making capabilities in the areas of demand, supply, and production planning and in other areas as well.

All the technologies work together toward achieving supply chain optimization, reducing overhead costs involved in transportation and storage, improving overall visibility and consequently allowing for faster response times. For example, consider the following situation:

> Company A is a B2C company that receives products from manufacturers and delivers them to the consumer. Company A will clearly have associated warehouse and transportation costs, among others. Company B is one such manufacturer that ships their product to Company A by air upon request. To provide better tracking information to the customer, RFID tags could be used, and products could be tracked in real-time. A decision support

system could be used for optimized route selection (a product of predictive analytics) based on distance and also on dynamic conditions such as weather. Any change in course by a Company B flight would need to be updated in real-time with Company A, and a cloud-based platform allows for just that. With the updated information, Company A could better coordinate ground transport once the shipment lands. An optimization algorithm could be employed for minimizing time and truck waiting costs as the product is transported to the warehouse operated by Company A.

Once the product enters the warehouse, an automated system will allow AGVs to take over, and transport it to the necessary aisle for storage. To minimize storage space required, and overall warehouse area, the warehouse would be optimally designed and may also be equipped with hi-tech systems such as smart glasses, to enable better warehouse maintenance. The RFID is still in function, and the customer is able to track location information in real time. Once the product is ready to be shipped, an automated warehouse management system would "talk" to an intelligent pick-and-place robot and update it on visual information of the product that needs to be selected from a pile. The robot's arm, equipped with a 3-D vision system, will be able to successfully sort and pick up the required product. The product would then be loaded onto a truck by an AGV, following packaging, and shipped to the customer. Alternatively, in the near future, drones would automatically latch on to the product, and fly it to the customer in time. It must be noted that the customer would be able to track the product in real-time, as the RFID tag is still in function, until it reaches their doorstep.

A major barrier to adopting new technologies in the supply chain is the lack of a business case to justify investment [2]. Here, the major challenge is to cost-justify investing in new technologies and capabilities to improve the ability to address the greater variability in customer demand patterns. Figure 2.2 suggests that a redesigned supply chain network may be required, since cloud computing, used together with analytics, can provide opportunities for greater end-to-end real-time/near-real-time visibility across supply chain partners. Such visibility enables multienterprise or multitier collaboration with supply chain partners while maintaining efficiency and improving performance, and ultimately reducing business and partner risk.

Emerging markets can pose additional barriers for new technology, due to volatile conditions that can complicate growth and production. While companies favor using new technologies in their current market supply chains, companies are not using technology extensively in emerging markets, automating only some essential processes [7]. Companies with leading high-performance supply chains tend to use technology more extensively in emerging markets than lower performers, since leading performers are twice as likely to achieve at least 20 percent growth in these markets in 2 years.

Technology is ever-changing. Supply chains must account for this and be adapted accordingly. A chain is only as strong as its weakest link, and not allowing for dynamic transformation in all sectors would only stagnate progress. It is hence not progress in one area, such as transportation or warehousing, that a company must look at but all areas in the supply chain. With an integrated system of technologies in place, advancements in any one sector, such as better optimization software or more accurate RFID tags, contribute to the health of the entire supply chain.

References

[1] Titze, C., R. Barger. 2015. Evolving Concepts in the Supply Chain Visibility. Gartner Report, January 19.
[2] Ricciarelli, A. 2015. Supply Chain Innovation—Making the Impossible Possible. MHI Industry Report, April 6.
[3] Project and Procurement Management Benchmark Report. 2014. Noosh, Inc.
[4] McKeefry, H.L. 2014. "Collaborative Sourcing Reduces Costs and Time." *EBN*. www.ebnonline.com
[5] Phillips, A. 2015. "Mobility, Collaboration and Transportation: Key Supply Chain Trends for 2015." www.supplychaindigital.com/supplychainmanagement/3745/Mobility-collaboration-and-transportation:-key-supply-chain-trends-for-2015/
[6] Maloney, D. 2015. "KPM Changes Its Fulfillment 'Landscape' with Voice." *DcVelocity*. www.dcvelocity.com/articles/20150212-kpm-changes-its-fulfillment-landscape-with-voice/ (accessed June 22, 2015).

[7] Degun, G. 2014. "Better Use of Technology Will Help Emerging Market Supply Chains, says Accenture." *Supply Management,* September, 10. www.cips.org/supply-management/news/2014/september/better-use-of-technology-will-help-emerging-market-supply-chains-says-accenture/

[8] Brown, S., A. Basu, T. Worth. 2010. "Predictive Analytics in Field Service." *Analytics Magazine,* November/December. http://analytics-magazine.org/predictive-analytics-in-field-service/

[9] Noyes, K. 2014. "The Shortest Distance Between Two Points? At UPS, It's Complicated." *Fortune,* July 25. http://fortune.com/2014/07/25/the-shortest-distance-between-two-points-at-ups-its-complicated/

[10] Rosenbush, S., L. Stevens. 2015. "At UPS, the Algorithm Is the Driver." *Wall Street Journal,* February 16. www.wsj.com/articles/at-ups-the-algorithm-is-the-driver-1424136536

[11] Imhoff, C. 2013. "Architecture Matters: Real-time In-memory Technologies Do Not Make Data Warehousing Obsolete." Intelligent Solutions Inc. www.sap.com/documents/2016/12/88529d63-9d7c-0010-82c7-eda71af511fa.html

[12] Haughwot, J. 2015. "Sensor Tech and IoT: Building the Intelligent Supply Chain." February 27. www.mbtmag.com/articles/2015/02/sensor-tech-and-iot-building-intelligent-supply-chain

[13] Press Release. 2010. "TMC's New Social Media Site Has Supply Chain Executives Talking—to Each Other" February 10. www.chrobinson.com/en-US/newsroom/Press-Releases/2010/02-10-2010_TMCs-new-social-media-site-has-supply-chain-executives-talking-to-each-other/

[14] McCrea, B. 2015. "Supply Chain and Logistics Technology: YMS Takes Flight." *Logistics Management,* April 1. www.logisticsmgmt.com/article/supply_chain_and_logistics_technology_yms_takes_flight

[15] Swedberg, C. 2009. "Two Food Chains Trial RFID-based Electronic Shelf Labels." *RFID Journal,* March 30. www.rfidjournal.com/articles/view?4737/

[16] Lee, H., K. O'Marah, G. John. 2012. "The Chief Supply Chain Officer's Report—2012." *SCM World,* October 19. www.supplychainmovement.com/the-chief-supply-chain-oofficer-report-2012/

CHAPTER 3

The Science of Inventory Optimization

Profit Optimally Managing Change and Variability in the Supply Chain

William E. Stillman

Written in memory of William C. Benton, one of the early pioneers of the Science of Inventory Optimization, the discoverer of many of its principles and methods, and the inventor of GAINS (General Adaptive INventory Solution).

Few will argue that one of the most challenging realities in the business world is dealing with constant change, variability, and error: customers change their minds; raw material deliveries show up late or are short on quantity; the forecast is in error; the stocking plan is in error; and so on. Half-in jest, we define the cause for all this change, error, and variability as "Murphy's Law": "Whatever can go wrong, will go wrong." Although we expend great effort in trying to minimize the negative financial impacts of "Murphy's Law," we have not been successful in eliminating it or managing it. For most companies we actually accommodate it by enabling inventory write offs, physical and financial buffers, and setting up actual budgets to accommodate a prescribed cost of expediting.

All of these accommodations and buffers are based on a plan, as is almost everything in business. In order to control the business against a finite financial amount of money, we set up production plans, inventory policies, replenishment plans, distribution plans, and so on. Then we try

to effectively manage these plans. Unfortunately, error, change, and variability get in our way. We miss our targeted plans and either spend more
money trying to correct for "Murphy" and miss earning more money
because "Murphy" results in lost orders.

As with anything in the business world, if you want to achieve targeted
objectives and do so in a certain time frame, against certain specifications,
under certain conditions, with a maximum contribution to margin, you
need to create a plan to do so. You then need to manage circumstances to
ensure that the plan is followed and its objectives are achieved. Managing
a company's supply chain is no different. Simply put, a corporate supply
chain is that flow of inventory or goods that delivers a requested product
to a customer on the day requested in the size, shape, color, and so on,
the customer requested. The ultimate goal in this process is to achieve
the "perfect order," that order, which meets all customer parameters and
specifications, is delivered exactly as requested, and maximizes the contribution to the order creator's margin.

This issue has challenged the executive suite for years. Corporations
have spent hundreds of millions of dollars on outside consulting firms and
enterprise software trying to manage the impact of "Murphy" on their
inventory investment and operating costs. All to no avail. According to the
2015 annual report issued by the Council of Supply Chain Management
Professionals (CSCMP), the inventory-to-sales ratio, which measures a
business' inventory investment in relation to its monthly sales, rose rapidly
in 2014. The ratio ended in 2014 at 1.35, its highest level since late 2009.
A rising ratio generally indicates declining sales or excess inventory levels.
What is even more interesting is that from 2000 to 2009, according to the
U.S. Census Bureau, Department of Commerce, the ratio had remained
essentially flat, vacillating between 1.4 and 1.3. According to Gartner
Group, the last 20 years has also seen the greatest growth in enterprise
software investment in history. All of that investment in tools intended
to improve inventory investment or operational efficiency; and yet, little,
if any, industry average improvement was documented (specific companies may have documented improvement but on average manufacturers
received little ROI from their software and consulting project investments).

The reason for this is twofold. In order to deal with the complexities
of "Murphy," the corporate and the consulting world segmented the overall problem into what they perceived as "manageable" pieces and built

projects and methods around each piece. There was a project for solving the forecasting issues, another project for solving the demand planning issues, another project for warehousing issues, another for the distribution network, another one for production, and so on. What no one recognized at the time was that the problem could not be optimally solved in silos. The reason is that silos or various parts are interdependent and need to be solved simultaneously, across the enterprise.

The second challenge, related to such interdependence is that no one had tools that could support resolution of an enterprise-wide problem where the interdependence of so many variables required the simultaneous, comprehensive analysis and resolution, in an environment that was constantly changing. The segmented silo approach, by its very nature, added incremental error and variability to the enterprise problem as a whole, thus further ensuring more error. More error correlates to more cost.

Remember, all of this effort and expense is expended in an effort for management to achieve the "Perfect Order."

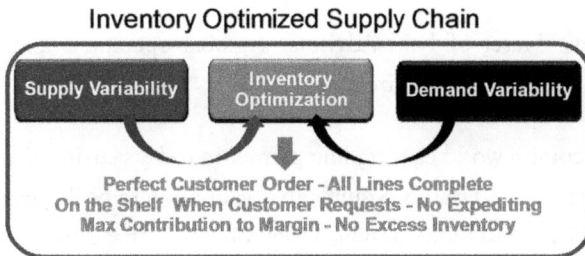

Inventory Optimized Supply Chain

In order to consistently achieve the "Perfect Order," with the maximum contribution to margin, one needs to plan across the enterprise at the most granular level. This means planning at the item or SKU level for every location (SKUL) where inventory is held or used. In some of his original research on inventory behavior in the supply chain, Professor William C. Benton of Purdue University realized that every SKUL in an enterprise can have a unique pattern of behavior and that that pattern of behavior changes at least once in a 10- to 14-week period. He further realized that in no two such periods does that change take place at the same time.

As Professor Benton continued his research, he also recognized that if one were to establish a plan to consistently achieve the "Perfect Order," one needed to account in that plan for all variables and needed to monitor the enterprise to identify any changes in SKUL behavior patterns, customer behavior patterns, or other relevant elements of the enterprise supply chain. In addition, one needed to forecast and plan around comprehensive error and variability with the objective of being able to manage that comprehensive error.

These two discoveries, the need to forecast and analyze at the SKUL level across the enterprise and the need to plan and manage comprehensive error and variability including all costs, constraints, dependencies, and so on, formed the foundation of the Science of Inventory Optimization (IO) for which Professor Benton was one of the early practitioners.

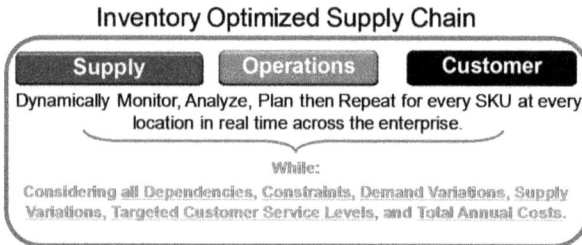

Inventory Optimized Supply Chain

Supply	Operations	Customer

Dynamically Monitor, Analyze, Plan then Repeat for every SKU at every location in real time across the enterprise.

While:

Considering all Dependencies, Constraints, Demand Variations, Supply Variations, Targeted Customer Service Levels, and Total Annual Costs.

As Julie Fraser of Iyno Advisors, a global operations and strategy consulting firm, has recognized:

> To become a world class trading partner in today's environment of change and uncertainty requires an organization to be diligent and proactive in real time planning. Only companies that can effectively plan and manage their supply chain can reach their full financial potential. With change becoming the new constant, supply chain planning is critical; companies must build a full-time center of excellence that can deliver plans and updates in real time [1].

That said, even the best supply chain plans often do not achieve their objectives. The colloquial quip, "stuff happens," is all too often part of the executive vernacular. The primary reason these plans are not met is that the planning methods and tools used do not get granular enough nor are they able to dynamically monitor and replan in real time.

The division of labor that has worked until now—such as demand, inventory, or production planning—has actually impeded our ability to optimize because optimization needs to fully and con-currently consider impacts across every SKU in every location in every phase of the supply chain. Our brains are not wired to handle that, but fortunately some software developers have been able to create dynamic tools and suites of algorithms that follow the rules and principles of the Science of Inventory Optimization, states Julie Fraser of Iyno Advisors [2].

The Science of IO ensures supply chain plans are both profit opti-mized and as highly accurate as possible.

The Science of IO treats the supply chain as one, contiguous, homo-geneous entity. It is not broken up into silos or fiefdoms that operate uniquely and can be planned uniquely and then, through some form of collaboration, fused together. The Science states that all elements/components of the enterprise are interdependent and linked. You can-not affect demand without affecting supply. You cannot affect replen-ishments without affecting costs. You cannot affect inventory policies without impacting customer orders, and so on. The Science of IO envelops every aspect of the enterprise where any piece of inventory rests or passes through. When management plans to deliver the "Perfect Order," they need to incorporate, comprehensively, every element of the enterprise simultaneously. Because, every component of the enterprise, down to the smallest SKUL (stock-keeping unit by location), is subject to change at any time. Therefore, to consistently achieve the "Perfect Order," management needs to comprehensively Monitor, Analyze, and Plan (MAP) all policies, plans, and actions for the enterprise, at every SKUL level, every day.

William C. Benton designed and built one of the very first IO solu-tions for Amway, over 40 years ago. In order to run the system, Amway had to lease time on the Cray Computer at the University of Michigan. Today, a robust laptop is able to run most IO solutions. With the early IO solutions, one had to build a database that contained the data the system needed in order to optimize inventory policies, demand plans, replenish-ment plans, distribution networks, and production plans. Today's leading edge ERP solutions already capture some 95 percent of the data required for IO. Cutting-edge IO solutions quickly and efficiently interface with such ERP solutions and they collect and format any data that may still be missing from the ERP solution.

To this point, we have talked about the capability of the Science of IO at a high level. Let us look at a more granular level as to some of the more specific functionalities a profit-optimized IO solution needs to have in order to achieve the profit optimal "Perfect Order."

Optimized Demand Planning and Forecasting

Forecasting is not a new concept to most of us. Its basics are well known. You take a period of time as your historic base, run that curve against a forecasting model and derive an expected demand pattern against which you try to project tomorrow's demand. What the Science of IO has identified, is that such granular forecasting is difficult to achieve without a supportive IO tool. Additionally, forecasting cannot be a standalone functionally. It needs to be an integral part of an entire IO tool, a tool that dynamically:

1. Forecasts at the lowest level: SKUL (sock keeping unit @ location).
2. Recognizes that every SKUL can change its pattern of behavior at least once every 14 months.
3. Recognizes that in no two periods does a pattern of behavior change at the same time.
4. Given the number of potential patterns of behavior possible, one needs to be able to select from some 40 or more forecast models to ensure that all potential behavior patterns are covered.

In order to achieve all these, given the thousands of items (SKULs) most companies have in their operations, this needs to be done dynamically. Given the potential frequency of pattern change, it also needs to be redone whenever a pattern change is detected that could have a financially significant impact on the company. These resulting forecasts need to be dynamically tested for plausibility—how well does the forecast fit the current and expected economic conditions? When conditions or behavior patterns change, what is the impact on the plan, costs, policies, and the total enterprise?

Pattern-Recognition Models

More than 40 pattern-recognition models are designed to automatically recognize observed demand patterns and predict a baseline future demand that matches those patterns. In his original research, Professor Benton built a dynamic model testing and selection process that evaluated about 110 potential models. The goal was to find that model, for each specific SKU at each location that provided the most plausible or best manageable demand pattern. Least error was not the goal. Contrary to popular belief, in an optimized environment, the objective is not necessarily to pick the model that provides the least error, rather to pick the model that most effectively enables the management of the error and its associated costs.

The dynamic IO solution that Professor Benton invented, called GAINS, General Adaptive Inventory Solution, dynamically evaluates some 40 potential forecast models in relationship to all other relevant variables and economic conditions.

Proven Forecast Model Library	Family	Description
	I	Straight Line / Moving Average
• 40 proven forecast models -11 categories	II	Zero or Simple Trend / Seasonal
• Dynamically Runs Models for every SKUL	III	Exponential Smoothing
	IV	Linear Regression
• Dynamically performs validation tests	V	Double Exponential Smoothing
• Dynamically simulates for plausibility	VI	Significant Trend / Seasonal
• Ensures Forecast Error is Manageable	VII	Low Volume
• Manageable Error is the foundation for	VIII	Sporadic Poisson Distribution
Profit Optimized Inventory Policy	IX	Low Volume Poisson Distribution
	X	Effort Based Models (Service Parts)
	XI	Attribute Based Models

Planning with Comprehensive Error

We have already addressed the concept of comprehensive error to some degree. As is detailed in the following chart, there is significantly more error in an enterprise than the traditional forecast error, which most

Need to Plan For Comprehensive Error

Based on a study of 50 manufacturing companies, comparing actual inventory counts to both planned and stated count, GAINSystems, Inc found these typical errors to exist-at-all companies.

PIPE	PIPE Units	Typical % Error	Unit Error	UNIT Error Range
Onhand	70	+/- 3%	+/- 2	
Replenishment Orders	120	+/- 11%	+/- 13	
Un-Shipped	-10	+/- 10%	+/- 1	
Forecast Demand	-100	+/- 50%	+/- 50	82% of total unit error
Service Stock	-30	+/- 80%	+/- 24	is in FD and SS
PIPE Value	50		+/- 90	+140 to -40

Source: GAINSystems, Inc. corporate archives.

leading edge, ERP-based planning systems measure. In order to plan a profit optimal, "Perfect Order," one needs to identify, analyze, and measure comprehensive error for every SKUL across the enterprise, simultaneously.

The objective in generating a forecast for each item/location is to anticipate the pattern of expected demand. In this manner, inventory plans can be developed to match the anticipated demand maintaining higher levels of inventory when higher demand is anticipated and less inventory when lower demand is anticipated. For example, Stuller Settings manufactures and distributes jewelry products that have a very high seasonal demand pattern (Christmas and Mother's Day). It is obviously necessary to plan to have a larger inventory investment available during the peak seasons than is necessary during the off-season. At the same time, Stuller's work force is comprised of highly skilled labor that cannot be idled. How does one match the work force to demand given seasonal variability, given the cost of high skilled labor, given the goal of the "Perfect Order?"

Now introduce a new product. How will this change tomorrow's demand pattern? How do I now plan for tomorrow's production? In all probability, the policies and plans now need to dynamically adjust for an upward trend in demand while the phase-out of a mature product will show a decline in demand. These patterns of behavior need to be anticipated to assure that the inventory investment is optimal.

Another example of unique demand patterns is the Royal Australian Airforce who uses IO for the planning of their service parts requirements.

Very low and sporadic demand patterns but very high service levels characterize service parts. The challenge is to have the cost-optimal inventory level available when the demand is required.

Once you have achieved a profit optimal demand plan or forecast, you now need to translate that into the profit optimal supply chain plan. This incorporates not only the demand plan but also the replenishment plan, distribution plan, production plan, and so on. Remember that all of these elements are integral to the delivery of the "Perfect Order."

Key Capabilities of a World-Class Inventory Optimization Solution

Leading Indicator Analysis

This analysis automatically determines likely shifts in historical demand patterns and auto-adjusts the baseline forecast; these leading indicators can include machine/fleet usage data in the equipment repair sector. Example indicators include:

- Macroeconomic indicators such as changes in housing starts, interest rates, vehicle purchases, and so on.
- Commodity price changes, and so on.
- Point-of-sale data.

In many cases, issues not directly associated with historical demand patterns may influence future demand. For example, a company may open additional distribution centers requiring additional inventory investment not anticipated in the historical demand patterns. A company that sells to the building products industry may be influenced by factors such as anticipated housing starts or interest rates or both. Anticipating these kinds of changes can help develop an optimal inventory plan to support the anticipated changes in the demand. Both the Australian Air Force and AAR, which provides a wide range of products and services for the aviation industry including maintenance, repair and overhaul of commercial and military aircraft, use this functionality to plan optimally to have parts available to meet the planned schedules.

Inventory Optimization Case Study

- •$186 million reduction in spares inventory.
- •42% reduction of warehouse items held.
- •15% increase in service levels.
- •70% reduction in logistics workload.

" ... we saved over $16 million in operating costs our first year while reducing AOGs by 50%. We are used to having people promise such results, GAINS actually delivered."

Commanding Officer, RAAF Logistics Command

(AOG: Aircraft on Ground – Out of Service)

New-Item Management

New-item management is used for superseding (direct replacements), similar (mostly similar attributes), related (some similar attributes), and entirely new product launches.

The introduction of new products presents additional challenges because no historical demand patterns may exist for demand planning purposes. New items can be replacements for existing products, in which case, the patterns of demand for the replaced part can be used as a guide to initiate the plan for the new part. The other extreme is where the

Inventory Optimization Case Study

- • 11% increase in EBIT during first 12 months
- • $60 million sales increase,
- • No additional inventory investment
- • 97+% "on shelf" item availability with no expediting
- • $12 million improvement in operating cash flow within 12 months
- • Capacity management through peak periods levelled 'business as usual' for warehousing & logistics departments during Christmas

With over 290 retail auto parts stores and 10 distribution centers, Super Cheap is the largest after-market auto parts distributor in Australia. "We have strategically grown our business by having the broadest selection of parts with the highest off the shelf service level in the industry. 97% off the shelf availability when the customer walks in the door allows us to provide next day delivery on the special orders that comprise the remaining 3%."

VP Operations

product is entirely new. In this case, an estimated pattern of demand can be used to initiate the plan and then is closely monitored as the actual demand is captured. Australian-based Super Cheap Auto sells automotive parts and accessories, which are characterized by a large volume of new products introduced on a regular basis. Because of the dynamic nature of that business, they use IO for forecasting on a weekly basis to assure that they are responsive to market needs.

Cross-Department and Cross-Enterprise Collaboration

Collaboration can be used to include "extrinsic" or market knowledge into the forecast (that cannot effectively be captured via Leading Indicators). This includes:

- Ability to manage workflow across multiple groups in the organization (e.g., Marketing, Sales, Finance, Operations).
- Ability to share demand (or replenishment) plans with suppliers and customers for notification, validation, and refinement.

This functionality provides for the inclusion of market-type knowledge, which is not available through leading indicator analysis. It also provides for input from company organizations such as marketing (e.g., promotions), sales (e.g., price changes), operations (e.g., plant shutdown), and so on. The system then also provides for sharing the resulting demand

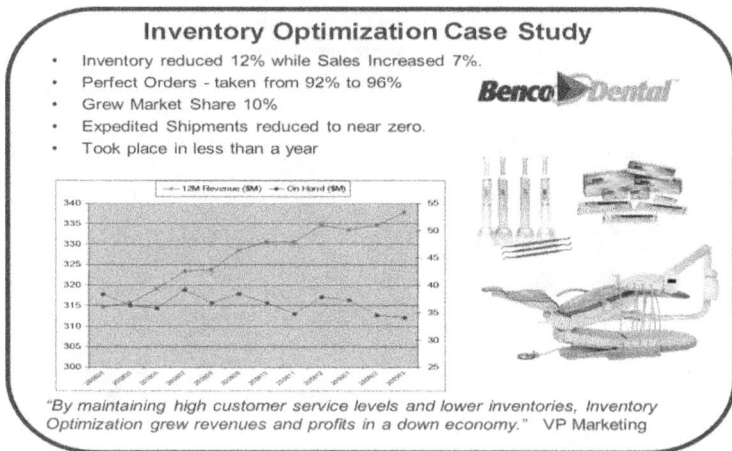

Inventory Optimization Case Study

- Inventory reduced 12% while Sales Increased 7%.
- Perfect Orders - taken from 92% to 96%
- Grew Market Share 10%
- Expedited Shipments reduced to near zero.
- Took place in less than a year

Benco Dental

"By maintaining high customer service levels and lower inventories, Inventory Optimization grew revenues and profits in a down economy." VP Marketing

plans with suppliers and customers to properly communicate anticipated results. Benco Dental, a major supplier of dental supplies, finds this functionality quite beneficial to support their monthly promotions to their more than 20,000 customers.

Multiechelon Stocking Policy Optimization

These are algorithms that determine whether to stock an item and at what service level to stock each item given the:

- Impact on total costs or profit or both.
- Interdependencies among locations (at the same or different levels in the network).
- Interdependencies within a bill-of-material (BOM) such as where-used, density, critical-path-likelihood, cumulative lead-time, and so on, to devise "postponement strategies."
- Customer expectations.

There are a number of factors that influence what, where, and in what quantities to stock. This functionality takes into consideration the service-level objective as well as the cost-optimal service level, cost and profit impact of stocking policy, product interdependencies between stocking locations, interdependencies within a bill-of-material including where-used dependencies, critical path likelihood, cumulative lead-time, and so on, and customer expectations (e.g., stocking minimums).

Inventory Optimization Case Study

- Inventory reduced by 27% in first year.
- Operating costs reduced by 23%.
- Line item fill rate maintained at 99%.
- Implemented & tracking benefits in 10 wks.

S T U L L E R

Inventory Optimization has not only enabled us, for the first time in history, to consistently achieve our targeted service levels, but we have done so with 27% less inventory than our ERP system recommended. This has helped us quickly grow our bottom line. Due to GAINSystems' professional approach to implementation, we were live in 10 weeks.

Vice President of Logistics

Stuller Settings finds this functionality extremely beneficial because of the dependency of raw materials, rings, settings, and stones of their jewelry products. In addition, O'Neal Flat Roll, a leading flat-roll steel service center, uses this functionality to maintain optimal steel coil inventories in addition to the converted sheets.

Inventory Policy Optimization

This considers a comprehensive set of planning error sources to identify the optimal ordering sizes and buffer stock including consistently achieved targeted service levels. These error sources include:

- Demand plan/forecast error
- Lead-time variation
- Yield/quantity-delivered performance
- Optimal ordering cycles (considering ordering constraints as well as price breaks).

In order to develop the optimal reorder quantity, this functionality considers a variety of factors. These include the forecast/demand plan error, lead-time variation (difference between when the product was expected vs. when it was received), yield/quantity received variation (quantity ordered vs. quantity received), as well as ordering constraints (when will product be available). In addition, price breaks (the more ordered, the less the unit cost but the higher the carrying cost) are also considered. Mayer Electric, a major distributor of electrical supplies with 5 distribution hubs, 45 stocking branches, and 300,000 SKULs, finds this functionality invaluable in optimizing their inventory investment. In addition, Benco Dental, with more than 90,000 SKULs, utilizes this functionality to assure that they are getting proper price breaks from their suppliers.

Service-Level Optimization

This approach automatically determines service levels uniquely for each item to achieve an aggregate target while minimizing or maximizing a business objective. For example:

- Determining the mix of service levels by-item to deliver total service of 98 percent with minimum inventory investment.
- Determining the mix of service levels by-item to deliver maximum service while maintaining a specific inventory investment, inventory turnover, or purchasing budget.

In addition to determining the inventory investment required to meet service-level objectives, this functionality can establish the mix of service levels by-item to attain an overall service-level objective, as well as determine the mix of service levels by item to achieve a specific inventory investment, inventory turnover target, or purchasing budget. Aerodyne Alloys, an O'Neal Steel company, uses this functionality to determine the optimal service level at which to stock their specialized alloy products. Benco Dental uses this functionality to help them make stocking/non-stocking decisions.

Routing (i.e., Network-Flow) Optimization

Routing optimization considers which supplier provides lowest *total* cost and, in multisite environments, how to plan the flow of product through the network that considers:

- The inventory savings of hub-and-spoke (via buffer-stock pooling).
- The rehandling and transportation cost savings of direct-from-supplier shipping.
- The hybrid advantages of "cross-dock" logistics.

In multisite environments, this functionality plans the flow of product through the distribution network considering potential inventory savings with a hub-and-spoke environment, potential benefits with direct-from-supplier shipping, and potential advantages of "cross-dock" logistics (reconciling differences between potential demand, when product is ordered, versus actual demand, when product is received). Steel service centers find this functionality of great value in optimizing shipments from large vendors who have minimum purchase requirements to their distribution hubs, spokes, or direct shipments or both.

Sourcing Optimization

Determines the supplier(s) that provide the lowest *total* cost considering:

- Ordering minimums and volume-discounts (line and cross-item/order level) considering the level of demand
- In-bound logistics costs
- Lead time and lead-time performance
- Procurement costs.

Where multiple suppliers for the same part(s) are available (e.g., local vs. offshore), this functionality helps determine which supplier(s) provide the lowest total cost considering minimum order sizes and volume discounts, in-bound logistics costs, lead-time variability costs, and procurement costs. Several uniform suppliers in the United States use this functionality to balance their offshore and domestic suppliers, preferring the offshore due to cost but maintaining local sources to accommodate volatile demand requirements. Benco Dental also uses this approach to assist them in making stock/nonstock decisions.

Key Capabilities of a World-Class Replenishment Optimization Solution

New Order Creation, Prioritization, and Auto-Approval that considers lead-time requirements, likelihood of stock out, optimized order quantities, and auto-approval risks-versus-benefits.

This functionality generates the production/purchase order for the previously calculated optimal order quantity and can consider lead-time requirements and risks versus benefits of auto-approval when the product arrives. Benco Dental uses this functionality to approve automatically 75 percent of the purchase orders. This significantly reduces the associated operating costs.

Transfer Order Prioritization and Creation that considers parent–child, for example, headquarters-division relationships and, in instances of shortage, allocates as needed to minimize risk-of-stock out.

This function considers the parent–child relationship of ordered parts and will reallocate as needed to minimize the risk of stock outs. Mayer Electric uses this functionality to optimize their inventory investment across 5 distribution hubs and 45 stocking branches.

Optimized Redistribution that considers carrying costs of excess as well as on order inventory to preclude new supply orders when unnecessary. This approach considers the cost of excess stock as well as on order stock to preclude the processing of new supply orders when not necessary. This functionality is used by Mayer Electric and Hagemeyer to "share" inventory across their individual distribution networks.

Inventory Optimization Case Study

- 18% Reduction in Finished Goods Inventories.
- Increased "Perfect Order" fulfillment 96% to 98%.
- Synchronized inventory policies and planning world wide.
- Improved global inventory turns 20%.

THE **HILLMAN** GROUP™

"Through GAINS inventory optimization support, we were able to reduce inventories and eliminate a warehouse while simultaneously increasing our turns and customer service levels. GAINS enabled us to achieve service levels with significantly less inventory than our ERP tool did."

Vice President, Operations

Optimized Component Allocation. In instances of component shortages, this approach allocates components to multiple later-stage items to minimize finished goods stock outs across the entire network (i.e., allocation optimized across multiple echelons). In situations where there are shortages of components, this functionality will allocate the available components to those items that are in later stages of assembly in order to minimize finished goods (and costlier) stock outs. Niagra Lasalle Corp. uses this functionality to determine whether available bar stock or coil stock is the optimal source for meeting their customers' requirements.

Inventory Optimization Case Study

NIAGARA LASALLE CORPORATION

- Leading producer of cold-finished steel bar.
- Industry exhibits price volatility and sporadic sales patterns.
- Complicated environment with numerous interdependencies between raw materials and finished goods.

Inventory Optimization

- Implemented base solution
- Synchronized finished goods with raw materials in multi-echelon environment.
- Provided ability to quickly review forecasts and respond to changes in demand.

Results

1 year after implementation:

- 33% decrease in inventory.
- 10% increase in sales.
- Consistently high service levels.

Cross-Dock Optimization that dynamically redetermines target locations for in-bound supplies to the hub location. This function optimally reconciles the difference between the target demand locations for product when it was ordered versus the current demand locations when the product is received. Because of the multiple stocking locations and high service level requirements, Mayer Electric has found this functionality of key value.

Inventory Optimization Case Study

- Reduced active inventory 27% while maintaining industry leading service levels

- Reduced planning and receiving activity by 24% so team could focus more time on customer support during a slow economy

- Dropped over $2,000,000 to the bottom line in less than 12 months from go live

MAYER ELECTRIC SUPPLY

"Inventory Optimization's comprehensive error analysis and dynamic forecasting enabled us to effectively anticipate market decline and reduce our inventory investment on the right items, in the right locations, ahead of the economic slowdown. This not only dramatically reduced potential excess, but now has positioned us to have the right inventory, at the right location, at the right customer service level, as the economy comes back."   Vice President, Operations

Rotables Planning Optimization (MRO/Warranty). These are parts that can be rebuilt or overhauled. This approach considers unique repair parts planning needs such as:

- Core/carcass reverse logistics
- Variable repair times
- Capacity constraints
- Repair yields and requirements to "refresh" the rotable pool with new purchases
- Potential "zero-sum" rotable pool constraints/parameters
- Compliance with performance-based logistics (PBL) requirements, which is an outcomes-based product support strategy.

A major IO market is repair parts planning. Some of the unique requirements of this industry include the planning of the repair/rotable items, also termed *core/carcass reverse logistics*. Some of the variables that IO plans for include variable repair times based on what requires fixing, capacity constraints where a production center is also used for repair work, and the need to replenish the rotable inventory pool with new purchases. Some of the companies that use IO for their repairs planning include AAR, Bell Helicopter, and Gulfstream Aerospace.

Inventory Optimization Case Study
Bell Helicopter TEXTRON

- Reduced active spares19% as sales increased.
- Reduced Operating Costs 30%
- Maintained 98% off the shelf availability
- Eliminated conflicts between Repair and Manufacturing
- Ensured compliance with PBL requirements
- 8% increase in service parts sales.

"Bell Helicopter has been recognized as having the best customer service in the industry for many years, even before we installed GAINS. Now that GAINS is installed, however, we are able to provide the best service in the industry with 19% less inventory and 30% lower handling costs."

Manager, Support Systems Development

Automated and Optimized Order Pooling that builds multi-item and potentially multilocation orders that minimize the cost related to meeting supplier constraints (e.g., minimum value, full-container, etc.). Where replenishment planning can include multiple items for multiple locations all from the same vendors, this functionality builds multiple item/location orders to take advantage of supplier constraints including minimum value, full container, and so on. Both industrial distributor Hagemeyer and steel service center Metalwest use this functionality to optimize their purchase requirements.

Optimized Expediting and De-Expediting that considers the costs/benefits of actions to focus attention on high-impact actions often obscured by low-value-added "noise." This functionality provides focus and priority to those actions that have high benefits in relation to costs to keep them from being obscured by low-value-added "noise." For example, if O'Neal Flat-Roll is expecting product from an offshore source in six weeks, and the demand for that product has been rescheduled to a future period, this functionality will determine whether it makes sense to incur the cost of rescheduling the incoming product versus bringing it in as scheduled and incurring the additional carrying cost.

Inventory Optimization Case Study

- Reduced Inventory Investment by 25%.
- Significantly improved profit margins.
- Increased sales 4-5% due to a 15% increase in service levels
- IO Alerted us to market changes, caused by China, in time to react quickly and buy before a major price run up due to supply shortage.

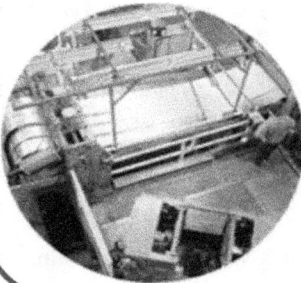

O'NEAL FLAT ROLLED METALS

"Based on a proof of concept analysis done prior to purchase, we were able to save $1million dollars by cancelling orders or changing the mix of orders to meet expected demand. Inventory Optimization paid for itself even before we signed our contract."

President and COO

"Rough-Cut" Production Capacity Optimization that optimally smooths orders in light of prebuild when needed (e.g., in seasonal environments) and allocates projected needs optimally during shortages. This functionality helps "balance" production requirements for those periods when capacity is available and cost-optimally allocates capacity for those

periods where there are excess demands. Steel processors such as Niagara LaSalle will use this functionality to balance their various steel-producing options equitably. Because of the high seasonality of the Stuller Settings business and the limited production capacity, they will use this functionality to optimize manufacturing of product during the "off season" so they have it available during the peak.

Cycled Production Management that optimizes inventory policy and ordering in light of fixed ordering cycles (e.g., batched production runs). In those manufacturing environments where ordering cycles are fixed (batched production runs for example), this functionality optimizes inventory policy and ordering to accommodate those environments. WIX Filter is an example of an IO user that utilizes this capability.

Inventory Optimization Case Study

- Reduced factory setups by 38%.
- Exceeded customer service levels with less inventory.
- Reduced active inventories by 15%.
- Dropped over $2.5 million to bottom in 12 months.

WIX
FILTERS

"By using Inventory Optimization to drive our factory with profit optimized inventory policies we reduce set ups by 38% and exceeded our targeted customer service levels. I was amazed at how quickly we were able to install and interface IO with our ERP solution so that we were live and tracking financial benefits in 8 weeks."

Distribution Manager, WIX Filters

Purchase Order Manager that facilitates web-based communication of initial orders as well as subsequent changes (expedite and de-expedite requests) in a prioritized and value-driven fashion.

This functionality supports web-based communication to suppliers of new orders (both purchasing as well as manufacturing) as well as changes (including expedite/de-expedite) to existing orders in a prioritized and value-driven fashion. In this manner, those items that are critical appear "at the top of the list." Stuller Settings has been the developer of this functionality and is the prime user. Benco Dental is starting to utilize this function as well.

Supplier Planning Portal that provides configurable and secure requirements forecasts to ensure supplier readiness and improved delivery performance (to drive lower costs for both parties).

Configurable requirements forecasts can be provided to suppliers (both purchasing as well as manufacturing) to give the supplier a "peek" at anticipated requirements that can then be used to help them in their planning, thus resulting in improved supplier readiness and delivery performance. Stuller Settings has been the developer of this functionality and is the prime user, and Benco Dental is starting to utilize it also.

Supplier Scorecard that provides detailed and objective performance measures in both absolute and relative (i.e., ranking) terms including estimating cost impacts of performance issues. This function provides measurement of supplier performance including yield (quantity of products ordered vs. received) as well as delivery (when products ordered vs. when received). This information can then show the cost impact of performance issues (i.e., how much additional inventory, and at what cost) has to be carried to accommodate poor supplier performance. Stuller Settings has been the developer of this functionality and is the prime user. Benco Dental is starting to utilize this function as well.

Operational Questions Your Inventory and Replenishment Optimization Solutions Should Be Able to Answer Dynamically

Purchasing/Supplier Management—Typical Issues/Applications:

1. Which supplier ensures my lowest cost operations considering:
   - Standard costs?
   - Supply yield variance?
   - Actual lead-time variance?
2. Is this opportunistic volume discount truly profitable?
3. What does this shipping delay cost me in added operational expense?
4. What does this shipping delay cost me in customer service delay?
5. Considering profit and customer service, with which vendor should I place this order to ensure we meet customer requests at the lowest cost?

6. What is my best mix of vendors, where I have multiple sources, to ensure that I hit targeted customer service levels and yet still maximize my contribution to profit?

Purchasing/Replenishment Planning—Typical Issues/Applications:

1. What size order quantity should I place to ensure that the company meets promised service levels?
2. What size order quantity should I place to ensure that the company operates at least cost?
3. When should I place the next order to ensure meeting company profit goals?
4. What size shipping container should I request for least-cost operations?
5. Which orders should I consolidate to ensure lowest cost achievement of promised customer deliveries?
6. How can I consolidate orders in order to minimize transportation costs and still ensure that my promised customer delivery dates are met 99.9 percent of the time?
7. When I order from my offshore supplier, am I required to order in full container loads? How do I determine what is the profit-optimal container mix for future demand when I have to calculate in volume?
8. When being required to order in full container loads or full truckloads, and I do not have an immediate need for a full load, how do I pull in expected future orders by cost and volume?

Inventory Planning and Management—Typical Issues/Applications:

1. How much space will be needed over the next 6 to 12 months for least-cost operations?
2. What is the least-cost stocking location for item "X" to ensure promised delivery?
3. Considering all costs (transport, set ups, expediting, etc.), what is the least-cost stocking plan, by location, to provide my targeted customer fill rate, all line items?
4. Which items are most cost-effectively stocked as subassemblies?
5. Which items are most cost-effectively handled as "cross-dock" items?

6. My company continues to grow; where should I put my next warehouse? What size should it be? What items should be stocked there? What impact does this have on my current locations and stocking plans?

Manufacturing/Production—Typical Issues/Applications:

1. What is my most cost-effective manufacturing lot size over the next six months?
2. How do I achieve the lowest set up costs while ensuring that targeted customer service levels are achieved against customer delivery dates?
3. How do I plan labor utilization against demand to ensure cost optimization?
4. Given current capacity, what should I manufacture and when to maximize profit?
5. Given my very seasonal demand and my capacity over the next six months, when and how many of each product should I manufacture to ensure I meet demand, don't create back orders, and ensure least-cost operations?
6. To compensate for seasonal demand, what should I manufacture now when I have excess capacity to ensure maximized profit and no future stock outs?

Financial Issues/Applications—Typical Issues/Applications:

1. How much cash do I need to budget over the next XX quarters to support my inventory investment requirements?
2. What are the incremental costs incurred each month due to supplier delivery delays or yield issues?
3. What are the incremental costs in expediting and inventory investment caused by capacity constraints?
4. Given expected sales growth, at what point do the incremental expediting costs and inventory investment costs warrant adding manufacturing or warehouse capacity?
5. What expenses can be reduced by consolidating our planning and purchasing into a centralized function?

6. What are our earnings improvements obtained by profit optimizing our distribution network?

7. What is the negative cash drain (cost) of allowing customer-dedicated inventory levels now that we can document a guaranteed customer service level?

Marketing and Sales—Typical Issues/Applications:

1. What is my profit-maximized customer service level for my "A" customers?

2. How does this customer's request for faster delivery impact profit margins?

3. If I use "service" as a strategic tool to win market share, what will it cost?

4. Does the value of lost sales at current customer service levels compared to the total costs of increasing service levels warrant trying to capture those lost sales?

5. Which region, customer, type of customer, and so on, costs the least to service?

6. How will a change in customer requirements impact our service level?

7. Given our current expected customer orders, what is the impact on our margins of offering this customer premium service?

8. What would the impact be on delivery if this customer changed their order?

9. I have an emergency customer need; how can I deliver this product at the least cost and still meet my customer's emergency delivery date?

References

[1] Interview with Julie Frasier, Iyno Advisors, 31 Capt. Murphy's Way, Cummaquid, MA 02637.
[2] Julie Frasier, ibid.

CHAPTER 4

The Demand Prediction of Location-Dependent Services

Fazle Karim and Houshang Darabi

Introduction

The goals of this chapter are twofold. First, it reviews the methods for demand forecasting. Secondly, it provides a comprehensive framework for the prediction of the demand of location-dependent services such as healthcare facilities, retail stores, banks, restaurants, and so on. The United States has the largest economy in the world in terms of nominal GDP (gross domestic product) [1]. The country contains over 20 million businesses, some of which are location-dependent service businesses. Location-dependent service businesses provide intangible products that are dependent on its location. Common examples of location-dependent businesses are hospitals, restaurants, and transportation services. Businesses all over the world are maturing and are being "dominated by service focused businesses" [2]. Many of these location-dependent businesses require accurate demand forecasts. Demand forecasting can save businesses money, while increasing their profit.

Accurate forecasting is becoming vital for survival and success of businesses. Demand forecasting is becoming the foundation of location-dependent services as it helps with marketing and revenue [3]. Since location-dependent services are constantly changing, demand forecasting can help with better management and planning.

A forecast is a prediction of events that have not been observed. These events tend to be uncertain and are hardly ever 100 percent accurate [3]. The more accurate these predictions are, the more effective business planning decisions become. Demand forecasting is the prediction of the possible demand for a good or a service by considering past events and trends of similar events. Hence, demand forecasting permits you to determine how, when, why, and how much demand there will be for a certain service or good. Some analysts use the term *sales forecasting* instead of demand forecasting as they have the same meaning [4].

According to renowned business analysts, Cundiff and Still, "demand forecasting is an estimate of sales during a specified future period which is tied to a proposed marketing plan and which assumes a particular set of uncontrollable and competitive forces" [5]. It has plenty of advantages for a business.

In the past decade, there has been an increase in patent filings for models and systems that evaluate the potential demand of a service or good required by an organization. It is then used to determine the best marketing areas. Patent 20030033195 by Bruce and Bunted developed a method that used a subject's demand, supply, market share, and geographical area to optimally place additional retail stores [6]. Zias and Cassanego filed a patent that used demographic information from a business to evaluate potential geographic areas of possible expansion [7]. Two other patents, U.S. 7,043,445 B2 and U.S. 7,412,398 B1, calculated demand using a geographical information system that tracked U.S. Census Block groups and travel time [8, 9]. Allstate Insurance Company filed a patent, 8,041,648 B2, which determines the best location for a retail establishment using geographical factors and financial information, such as the cost of building a new establishment [10]. Patent U.S. 6,298,328 B1, filed by Healy and Dunn, is a system to size a market for a product or service by providing forecast information based on the product, geographical area, market segment, and time period. The system is useful for telecommunications and energy industries [11]. As can be studied from these patents, demand forecasts can help predict optimal locations of different service businesses.

The remainder of this chapter is structured as follows. In the second section, we discuss the advantages and types of forecasting. In the third section, we briefly review the different forecasting methods. In the fourth section, we present a framework for the demand prediction of location-dependent services. In the fifth section, we show a real-world case study for the application of the presented framework. In the sixth section, we provide the conclusions and future research topics.

Advantages and Types of Forecasting

Forecasting Advantages

Some important advantages of forecasting are discussed as follows. Accurate demand forecasting permits businesses to produce demand for services and sales by allocating various resources, such as labor, equipment, and raw material, effectively [4]. By determining demand for certain services and sales, businesses will be able to provide these services and goods to customers in a manner that will satisfy them. Forecasting helps determine significant events that have occurred in the past to satisfy demand for services and sales [4]. Based on these events, businesses can avoid repeating, and, or avoiding mistakes they have made in the past.

Demand forecasting helps businesses understand trends in their services or goods better. This allows businesses to expect changes in the market and take precautionary measures if necessary (in case sales are predicted to drop). It also allows them to keep up with competition. By correctly predicting the demand for services or goods for the upcoming future, businesses will be able to determine the right amount of resources required [4]. They will be able to determine how many employees will be required in producing the right amount of services and goods for the customer. Service businesses will be better at managing work hours for hourly workers. Correct amounts of raw material could be purchased earlier at a cheaper rate [4].

Businesses require accurate demand forecasts to receive financing and investments. This is especially true for start-ups. Lenders and investors prefer to know the demand forecast for the service or good provided by the company for a certain amount of time [4]. Only with this knowledge can lenders and investors finance or invest in the business. In a macrolevel, demand forecasting can help governments or states, or both, determine whether imports are necessary to make-up for the possible deficit of certain supply [4]. However, if there will be a surplus in demand for a good or service, governments can use this information to determine how much of the good or service they should export.

Types of Forecasting

Forecasting can be classified into two groups: active forecasting and passive forecasting [3]. When given the assumption that a business requires a future change in its course of action, active forecasting prediction is used. In the case that the course of action will remain unaltered, passive forecasting is used.

Forecasting is also classified by time spans using long-term and short-term demand forecasting [3]. Normally, short-term forecasting is forecasting done when the time span is three months, six months, or a year, depending on the type of business. Short-term forecasting is used for determining short-term financial and marketing plans, setting sales targets, determining the price of service and goods, managing raw resources, and avoiding over production or short supply. Short-term forecasting emphasizes on seasonal patterns [4].

Long-term forecasting predicts goods or services demand during a time period of 5, 10, or 20 years [3]. Predicting the long-term demand of a good or service is much harder than predicting the short term as demand tends to fluctuate with a greater magnitude. Long-term forecasting is normally used when trying to expand or reduce the business, planning long-term financial and marketing plans, allocating the right amount of resources, and determining the direction the business needs to go toward [3]. Long-term forecasting helps the business with strategic planning [4].

Demand forecasting is also categorized by level of forecast [3]. These levels are macrolevel, industry level, firm level, and product-line level [3]. Macrolevel forecasting studies businesses and their impact on the economy [3]. Industry-level forecasting is forecasting that studies a particular market or industry [3]. Firm-level forecasting is forecasting that studies an individual firm and its managerial strategies [3]. Product-line forecasting is forecasting that studies a firm's individual products and its impact on the business [3].

Forecast Methods

There are many techniques used to forecast demand of location-dependent services. Figure 4.1 summarizes the different forecasting techniques.

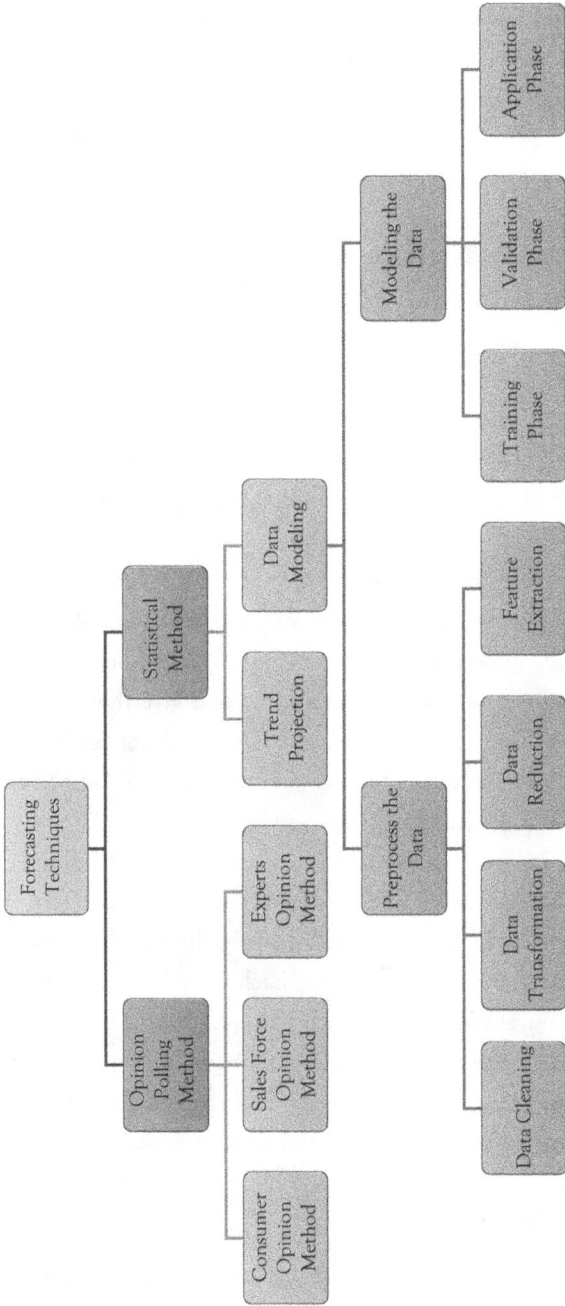

Figure 4.1 Summary of different forecasting techniques

Opinion Polling Method

One common way to forecast demand is by using the opinions of experts, buyers, and other significant players in the industry to better understand the emerging market and trends. There are three types of opinion methods used for demand forecasting: consumer survey, sales force opinion, and experts' opinion.

The consumer opinion method [4] is when the consumer is surveyed about their future ideas about the service/good. If the service/good is an intermediate service/good, then customers would be the other business. The customers are the ones responsible for forecasting demand. Typically, the opinions of customers are measured through door-to-door surveys, random household representative surveys, and through deducing the demand of its clients. One main advantage of this method is information being obtained first hand. Nevertheless, this method can end up being costly in terms of money and time.

The sales force opinion method [4] is when the sales people are surveyed about the future of the service/good. For example, in a restaurant, the sales force would be the waiters. This method is a bottom-up approach. Managers discuss these surveys and give their forecast of the service/good. The composite forecast is what the business uses. The main advantage of using this technique is it is cheap and easy. However, it bases a lot on the experience of the sales people.

The experts' opinion method [4] is when a panel of experts is interviewed and surveyed about the future of the service/good. This method is also known as the Delphi method. Normally, these experts are required to answer a sequence of questionnaires. Each set of questionnaires is developed based on answers of the previous questionnaire. This method can be beneficial in forecasting long-term demand, as experts tend to have experience in the particular industry. This method relies heavily on the opinion of the expert and can lead to biased forecasts.

Statistical Method

A very useful and commonly used method in demand prediction is the statistical method. Four common methods used in demand forecasting are trend projection, barometric, regression, and simultaneous equations [3, 4].

Trend projection [4] is the study of demand trends using trend lines, least square linear regression, exponential smoothing, and the moving average method. Trend lines are very easy to use and visualize as the trend line is the line that best fits the demand curve. Least square linear regression, exponential smoothing, and moving average are methods that used to help analyze time series trends [4]. Other machine learning algorithms, such as random forests, can be also used to forecast demand of services and goods.

The statistical algorithms developed/used for forecasting demand need to be robust and able to predict accurately. For accurate predictions, one must follow the following steps:

1. Preprocess the data
   a. Data cleaning
   b. Data transformation
   c. Data reduction
   d. Feature extraction
2. Modeling of the data
   a. Training phase
   b. Validation phase
   c. Application phase

Preprocessing data normally entails cleaning the data, transforming the data, and reducing the data [12]. It is an essential part when handling data. The process in which corrupt or inaccurate data are resolved is known as data cleaning. This is also where missing values in the dataset are designated a value, such as "NA," or "missing," or are imputed using different techniques [13]. The most common imputation method is by finding the mean of quantitative data, and the mode for qualitative data [14]. Other imputation practices can include using regression, K-NN, or other modeling techniques [14]. In addition to dealing with missing values, outliers are identified. Typically, outliers are removed from the dataset so that the models developed to predict demand are not skewed [13].

When studying data, it is sometimes necessary to transform the data [12]. It is common to transform the data when the data is skewed, such that data can be visualized better, the data has improved interpretability, and its confidence interval can have a better coverage probability. Common transformation techniques include transforming the data to a normal distribution [12], transforming the data to a uniform distribution [16], log transformation [15], square root transformation [15], or linear transformation [16].

A dataset can contain attributes or attribute values that are unnecessary, which can influence the model to predict demand negatively by making it less robust. Dimensionality reduction is the process in which the attributes or attribute values are condensed [17]. Some of the state-of-the-art dimensionality reduction techniques are missing value ratio (removal of data attributes that have missing values greater than a threshold), low variance filter (removal of normalized data attributes that have low variances), high correlation filter (reduction of normalized attributes that are highly correlated into just one attribute), principal component analysis (statistical procedure in which a new set of linearly uncorrelated variables is derived using orthogonal transformation on an existing dataset [19]), backward feature elimination (reduction of one attribute at each iteration to determine attributes that have the greatest impact on the prediction model), forward feature construction (addition of one attribute at each iteration to retain attributes that have the greatest impact on the prediction model), and random forest (sample of attributes at each iteration to determine a set of attributes that have the greatest impact on the prediction model) [18].

Once the data is preprocessed, the data needs to be partitioned randomly to avoid overfitting when determining the best prediction model for the dataset. If 100 percent of the data is used to develop the model, there is a greater likelihood that the prediction model will not be accurate in predicting future demand. In other words, the model tends to "memorize" the data and not learn from it [20]. This is known as overfitting. Overfit models are not able to predict unseen data using the model. If slight changes to the training data leads to drastic changes to the model, the model is overfitted [20]. To avoid this, it is necessary to have a validation phase after the training phase.

The training phase is the phase where the training dataset is used to fit a prediction model. It is important to use the right model depending on what the type of prediction is being done, regression or classification.

Table 4.1 Common models used for classification or regression problems or both

Model	Type
Adaptive Boosting [23]	Classification and Regression
Artificial Neural Network [25]	Classification and Regression
C4.5 [23]	Classification and Regression
Classification and Regression Trees (CART) [23]	Classification and Regression
Decision Tree [24]	Classification and Regression
K-NN [23]	Classification
Lasso Regression [26]	Regression
Linear Regression [24]	Regression
Logistic Regression [24]	Classification
Naïve Bayes [23]	Classification
Random Forest [24]	Classification and Regression
Ridge Regression [24]	Regression
Support Vector Machine (SVM) [23]	Classification

Regression is used when the dependent variable is continuous [21]. However, a categorical dependent variable, classification models are used [22]. Some of the common models used for classification and regression problems are shown in Table 4.1.

The validation phase is where the model that is fitted on to the training set is tested to see how well it performs with an unseen dataset, the testing set. Evaluating the model performance on the training set tends to be optimistic. To avoid overfitting there are two common methods used to validate models, Hold-Out and Cross-Validation [27].

The Hold-Out method is a method used for large datasets [27]. The data is randomly sectioned into three sets; training set, validation set, and testing set. The training set is a subset of the whole dataset where the model is fitted. The validation set another subset of the whole dataset where the prediction model fitted is tested and fine-tuned. Finally, the prediction model is tested on the testing set, an unseen subset of the whole dataset [27]. There are cases where models are developed without having a validation set. The training set contains about 40 to 60 percent of the whole data and remaining data is the testing set.

Cross-Validation method is used when the data available is limited [27]. To obtain an unbiased model performance, k-fold cross-validation is used. In k-fold cross-validation, a model is fitted k amount of iterations, with each iteration having a subset of the whole data for training and testing sets [27].

The performance of each model is measured depending on whether the model is a classification model or a regression model. For classification models, accuracy, precision, negative predictive value, sensitivity, recall, lift charts, gain charts, receiver operator characteristic (ROC) charts, Kolmogorov–Smirnov (K–S) charts, and area under the curve (AUC) curves can be used to evaluate the model [28]. Root mean squared error (RMSE), relative squared error (RSE), mean absolute error (MSE), relative absolute error (RAE), coefficient of determination, and standardized residual plots are used to evaluate regression models [29]. Table 4.2 depicts each of these methods.

Table 4.2 *Different methods used for model evaluation*

Method	Definition
Accuracy [28]	The percentage of correct predictions.
Precision, positive predictive value [28]	The percentage of the total positive predictions that were correctly predicted.
Negative predictive value [28]	The percentage of the total negative predictions that were correctly predicted.
Sensitivity or recall [28]	The percentage of actual positive cases that were correctly predicted.
Specificity [28]	The percentage of actual negative cases that were correctly predicted.
Gain chart [28]	A visual representation that depicts ratio between the results obtained with and without the predictive model. The gain chart has a y-axis of the percentage of positive responses and an x-axis of percentage of customers contacted.
Lift chart [28]	A visual representation that depicts ratio between the results obtained with and without the predictive model. The lift chart has a y-axis of the ratio between the results predicted by the model and when using no model, lift, and an x-axis of percentage of customers contacted.

Method	Definition
Kolmogorov–Smirnov (K–S) chart [28]	A visual representation that shows the degree of separation between positive and negative distribution. It is on a scale of 0 to 100 where 100 is in when two groups are completely separated into all positives and negatives. In other words, the higher the number, the better the model is in separating the positive and negative classes.
Receiver operator characteristic (ROC) charts [28]	The ROC chart is a curve with sensitivity as the y-axis, and 1-specificity (false-positive rate) as the x-axis.
Area under the curve (AUC) [28]	The AUC is the area under the ROC curve. A random curve has an AUC of 0.5 and a perfect model has an AUC of 1.
Root mean squared error (RMSE) [29]	A very common metric used for regression models. It is calculated through: $$\text{RMSE} = \sqrt{\frac{\sum_{i=1}^{N}\left(\text{Predicted}_i - \text{Actual}_i\right)^2}{N}}$$ where N is the total number of observations
Relative squared error (RSE) [29]	Another metric used in regression models. It is calculated through: $$\text{RSE} = \sqrt{\frac{\sum_{i=1}^{N}\left(\text{Predicted}_i - \text{Actual}_i\right)^2}{\sum_{i=1}^{N}\left(\overline{\text{Actual}} - \text{Actual}_i\right)^2}}$$ where N is the total number of observations
Mean absolute error (MAE) [29]	Another metric used in regression models. It is calculated through: $$\text{MAE} = \frac{\sum_{i=1}^{N}\left|\text{Predicted}_i - \text{Actual}_i\right|}{N}$$ where N is the total number of observations
Relative absolute error (RAE) [29]	Another metric used in regression models. It is calculated through: $$\text{MAE} = \frac{\sum_{i=1}^{N}\left|\text{Predicted}_i - \text{Actual}_i\right|}{\sum_{i=1}^{N}\left|\overline{\text{Actual}} - \text{Actual}_i\right|}$$ where N is the total number of observations

(Continued)

Table 4.2 Different methods used for model evaluation   (Continued)

Method	Definition
Coefficient of determination (R^2) [29]	The percentage of variance in the dependent variable that is predicted from the independent variable. The higher the R^2, the better the model.
Standardized residual plots [29]	A visual representation that depicts the residual plot, residual (observed-actual value) dispersion.

The application phase is the phase when the model is applied in the real world. The results of the data are used by the different players, such as businesses, industries, states, or governments. It is important for the model to be accurate, plausible, durable, flexible, available, and simple.

A Framework for Demand Prediction of Location-Dependent Service

There are many ways to predict demand. In this section, a framework to predict the demand of location-dependent service is introduced. The framework consists of two models—the physical model and the logical model. The objective of the framework is to predict the demand of location-dependent services at a micro and macrolevel.

Physical Model

To predict the demand of location-dependent services, quantitative data and qualitative data can be collected from multiple players and sources through different methods. Figure 4.2 show the different entities data can be collected to predict the demand of location-dependent services. The physical model is when all the data is collected from the different sources and linked with each other to create a large database, which will be used to predict the demand.

Logical Model

Once the physical model is completed, the logical model is developed. This is done in six steps. The logical model is used when calculating the demand for a location service in a systematic manner.

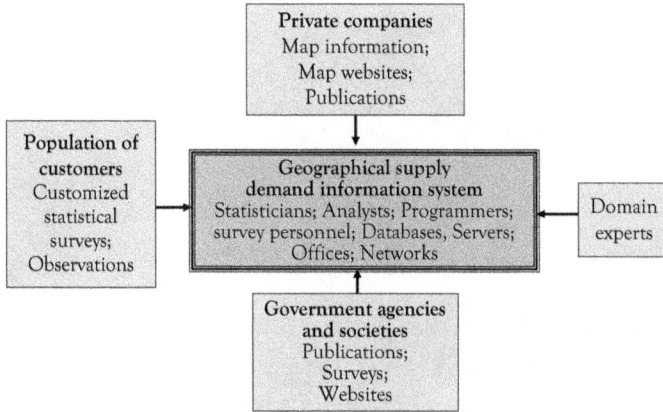

Figure 4.2 *Different entities where data can be collected to predict the demand of location-dependent services*

In the first step of the logical model, we define all the supply subjects that satisfy the independence property. The supply subject is an outcome/ product of a service that is purchased by customers of that service in some measurable units. For example, the restaurant service can have a supply subject of pizzeria, which is measured through the number of meals per week. The independence property states that all supply subjects defined for the same industry must not have any potential demand overlap. Hence the total potential demand generated for any two supply subjects is equal to the sum of the potential demand generated by each of them.

Once the supply subjects are defined and satisfy the independence property, we list all the demand generators for every supply subject by considering factors such as type, attribute, and location (Step 2). A demand generator is an entity that consumes the supply subject. For example, for a supply subject S (pizzeria), the demand generator can be a residential complex that uses local restaurants for fast food.

After listing the demand generators, we define possible supply subject locations (Step 3). A supply subject location is a geographical area in which a service provider can be established for the supply subject. Examples of a location can be shopping centers, an area defined by a zip code, a city, or a county.

The supply subject, demand generator for every supply subject, and supply subject location do not have members that overlap among the groups. The supply subject is a generic list, whereas the demand generator and location are physical; they correspond to some external entity.

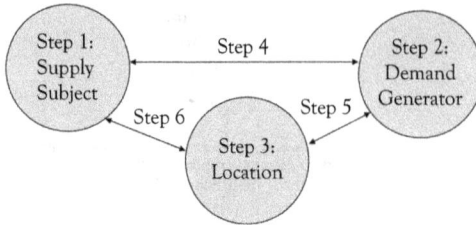

Figure 4.3 Summary of the logical model

Next, we predict the total demand of the supply subject generated by the generator for every generator supply subject (Step 4). We use the techniques listed in the third section to predict the total demand of the supply subject generated by the generator. Subsequently, we break down the total demand of a supply subject generated by every generator among all locations that can provide that supply subject (Step 5). Finally, for each location that can potentially provide a supply subject demand, we add all the predicted demand generated by each generator in that location. The summation is the total demand of the supply subject (Step 6). Figure 4.3 shows the summary of each step of the logical model.

Advantages of Using This Framework

The advantage of using this framework is that the demand of each supply subject can be viewed in a holistic manner. One can create a matrix that shows the demand of a supply subject from each generator in each location. This is useful as the demand for a location-dependent service can be viewed at a micro or a macrolevel. This framework can be extended into determining demand at a household level. The framework is adaptable to qualitative and quantitative data.

The transportation, food, and healthcare industries are industries that can benefit the most from this framework. For example, it is beneficial for hospitals to be able to predict the demand the possible demand the emergency room will have on a given night.

A Case Study for Prediction of Restaurant Services

The city of Naperville is home to many popular restaurants in Illinois. Naperville has over 2,000 restaurants. In the case study, we plan to

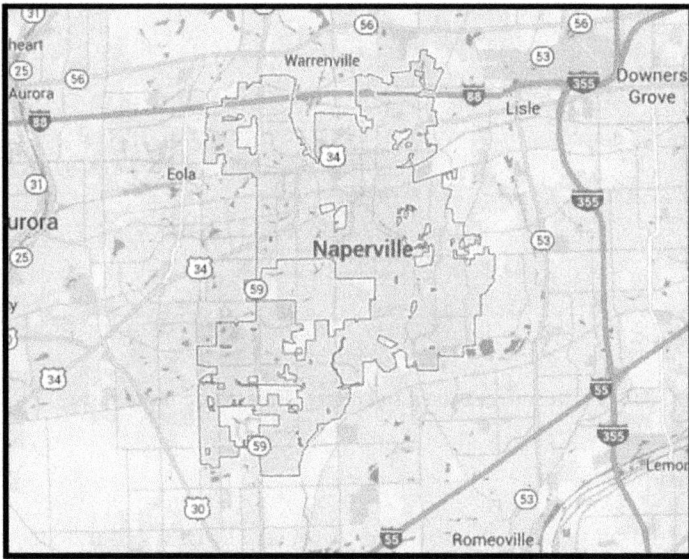

Figure 4.4 Map of Naperville, IL [30]

determine the demand for pizzeria in different areas of the city. A map of Naperville can be seen in Figure 4.4.

Physical Model

Initially, the physical model was used to collect the data. Figure 4.5 shows the data sources used to collect the data.

Some of the attributes collected from the physical model were latitude (of supply subject and demand generator), longitude (of supply subject and demand generator), household income, household size, time pizza was ordered, and type of pizza that was/were ordered. Customer surveys were used to collect data on favorite pizza type in different households, number of pizza they normally order, and when they would order a pizza (time of day and which day of the week), number of people in their household, address where they live (with latitude and longitude), and the gender of each household member. Restaurant owners, restaurant managers, and food experts were interviewed to collect information on what the different advertisements are being used, where they are being used, when the advertisement is active, and what pizza the advertisement promotes.

All the data was stored in a Microsoft Access database.

```
                    ┌─────────────────────────┐
                    │    Private companies     │
                    │ Google, Yahoo, at&t, Zillow│
                    └─────────────────────────┘
                                │
                                ▼
┌──────────────────┐    ┌─────────────────────────┐    ┌──────────────────┐
│   Population of   │    │   Geographical supply   │    │      Domain      │
│    Customers      │    │ demand information system│    │     experts      │
│     Surveys;      │──▶ │  Our personnel: Programmer,│   │ Restaurant owners,│
│  Observations on  │    │survey personnel, analysts, statisticians│ restaurant managers,│
│home consumptions in│   └─────────────────────────┘    │ and food experts │
│Naperville residential areas│           ▲               └──────────────────┘
│  based on family  │                    │
└──────────────────┘    ┌─────────────────────────┐
                        │   Government agencies    │
                        │     and societies        │
                        │   City of Naperville,    │
                        │   US Bureau of Census,   │
                        │National association of restaurants│
                        └─────────────────────────┘
```

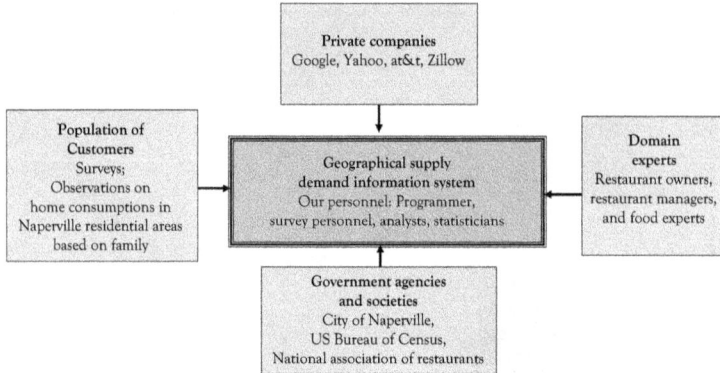

Figure 4.5 Data sources used to collect pizzeria demand data

Logical Model

Once the physical model was used to collect all the necessary data, the logical model was used.

The following steps were used to determine the demand of pizzeria in "Cell A," a notation showing a typical cell. Cell is defined as a nondisjoint area that all providers of the same service located there will have the same location effect on their demand.

Step 1:   There are about 30 supply subjects in Naperville with over 60 cells. Pizzeria was the supply subject.

Step 2:   Assuming the demand of pizzeria was to be calculated for Cell A, the demand generators were defined to be residential, business zones, people centers, passing-by customers. There are about 200 residential, 50 business zones, 100 people centers, and 30 passing-by customer demand generators (such as main streets that are used by travelers who are passing through the city).

Step 3:   Based on the distance and past information on where pizza was ordered, locations of potential demand generators for the particular pizzeria were determined.

Step 4:   For each combination of generator-subject, the demand forecast of the supply subject by the generator was calculated. To calculate the demand forecast, the data that was collected through the physical model was initially preprocessed.

The customer survey was preprocessed. Surveys that had over 75 percent missing values were removed. It was then noticed that the attribute for the gender of each household member had over 15 percent missing value. This attribute was removed from the dataset.

Based on the interviews of restaurant experts, the attribute type of advertisement being used did not vary as the local pizzeria mainly used flyers for promotion. Hence, this attribute was removed.

The remaining dataset that had information on latitude (of supply subject and demand generator), longitude (of supply subject and demand generator), household income, household size, time pizza was ordered, and type of pizza that was ordered, was merged into the restaurant interview section based on time (when the advertisement is active and when the pizza was ordered). Then the customer survey was merged on to the dataset based on latitude and longitude of each household from the survey and latitude and longitude of demand generator. Once all the data was put into one set, the missing values were imputed by finding the mode of quantitative data and the mode for qualitative data. Afterward, the data was clustered into weekly information, such that the demand of each supply subject was weekly. Once the data was split into multiple 10-folds with each having different training and testing sets, using R statistical software, different models were then used to fit the dataset and the random forest model was determined to be the best model (lowest RMSE score) in predicting the weekly demand.

Figure 4.6 summarizes the step-by-step process used to generate the demand forecast for each generator-subject combination.

Step 5: The demand forecast is then broken down into different locations.

Step 6: Locations that were very far away from the supply subject, or locations that never ordered from the supply subject were removed from the demand forecast list. The rest of the

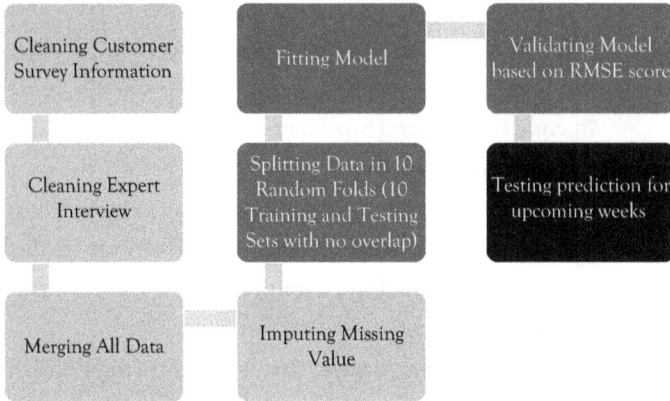

Figure 4.6 Step-by-step process used to generate the demand forecast for each generator-subject combination

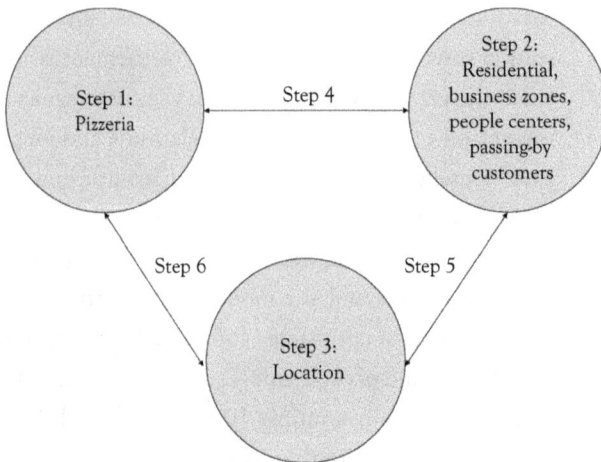

Figure 4.7 Logical model used for pizzeria case study

demand was summed up to find the total demand for the supply subject in Cell A.

To find the total demand of pizza from pizzeria per week in Naperville, the demand of each cell can be summed up. Figure 4.7 reviews the logical model used in this case study.

Conclusions and Future Research

In this chapter, we reviewed multiple demand prediction methods. We also presented a framework for demand prediction of location-dependent services. This framework is very robust and can easily determine demand forecast on a macro or microlevel. A matrix can be created to show the demand of a supply subject from each generator in each cell location. The framework can be used to determine demand from each household as it is able to adapt to quantitative and qualitative data.

For future research directions, one could apply the same framework to predict the demand generated by other location-dependent services in a given area. These services include but not limited to transportation, hospitals, banks, and retail stores. This framework is dynamic and beneficial to multiple players in the industry.

References

[1] Bajpai, P. 2016. "The World's Top 10 Economies." *Investopedia*. Retrieved June 30, 2016, from www.investopedia.com/articles/investing/022415/worlds-top-10-economies.asp

[2] Frei, F.X. 2008. "The Four Things a Service Business Must Get Right." *Harvard Business Review* 86, no. 4, pp. 70–80.

[3] Chand, S. 2014. "Demand Forecasting: It's Meaning, Types, Techniques and Method | Economics." Retrieved June 30, 2016, from www.yourarticlelibrary.com/economics/demand-forecasting-its-meaning-types-techniques-and-method-economics/28607/

[4] Jain, T.R., M.L. Grover, V.K. Ohri, and O.P. Khanna. 2007. "Demand Forecasting." In *Economics for engineers*, pp. 99–109. FK Publications.

[5] Still, R.R., and E.W. Cundiff. 1958. *Sales Management: Decisions, Policies, and Cases*. Prentice-Hall.

[6] Bruce, D.E., D.S. Bunten. 2003. Retail Site Location Void Analysis System and Method. US Patent 20030033195, filed June 5, 2002, and issued February 13, 2003.

[7] Zias, J.A., D.E. Cassanego. 2012. Method and System for Evaluating Expansion of a Business. US Patent 8,095,412 B1, filed 29 November 2011, and issued December 11, 2012.

[8] Bailey, W.G. 2006. Market Determination System. US Patent 7,043,445 B2, filed April 10, 2003, and issued May 9 2006.

[9] Bailey, W.G. 2008. Method for Analyzing Net Demand for a Market Area Utilizing Weighted Bands. Patent US 7,412,398 B1, filed September 17, 2001, and issued August 12 2008.

[10] Rossmark, S., K. Littlejohn. 2011. Retail Location Services. US Patent 8,041,648 B2, filed July 18, 2006, and issued October 18, 2011.

[11] Healy, E.M., G.T. Dunn. 2001. Apparatus, Method, and System for Sizing Markets. US Patent 6,298,328 B1, filed March 26, 1998, and issued October 2 2001.

[12] Han, J., J. Pei, and M. Kamber. 2011. *Data Mining: Concepts and Techniques.* 3rd ed. US: Morgan Kaufmann Elsevier.

[13] Larose, D. T. 2014. *Discovering Knowledge in Data: An Introduction to Data Mining.* 2nd ed. US: John Wiley & Sons.

[14] Brown, M.L., and J.F. Kros. 2003. "Data Mining and the Impact of Missing Data." *Industrial Management and Data Systems* 103, no. 8, pp. 611–21.

[15] Hand, D.J., H. Mannila, and P. Smyth. 2001. *Principles of Data Mining.* London: MIT press.

[16] Krzysztof, J.C., W. Pedrycz, W.S. Roman, and A.K. Lukasz. 2007. *Data Mining: A Knowledge Discovery Approach.* Berlin, Germany: Springer.

[17] Sorzano, C.O.S., J. Vargas, and A.P. Montano. 2014. "A Survey of Dimensionality Reduction Techniques." *arXiv*:1403.2877.

[18] Seven Techniques for Data Dimensionality Reduction. 2015. Retrieved June 30, 2016, from www.knime.org/blog/seven-techniques-for-data-dimensionality-reduction

[19] Neto, J. 2013. Principal Component Analysis. Retrieved June 30, 2016, from www.di.fc.ul.pt/~jpn/r/pca/pca.html

[20] Runkler, T.A. 2016. *Data Analytics: Models and Algorithms for Intelligent Data Analysis.* Berlin, Germany: Springer Science and Business Media.

[21] Introduction to Regression. 2007. Retrieved June 30, 2016, from http://dss.princeton.edu/online_help/analysis/regression_intro.htm

[22] Aggarwal, C.C. 2015. *Data Mining: the Textbook.* New York, NY: Springer.

[23] Wu, X., V. Kumar, J.R. Quinlan, J. Ghosh, Q. Yang, H. Motoda, G.J. McLachlan, A. Ng, B. Liu, S.Y. Philip, and Z.H. Zhou. 2008. "Top 10 Algorithms in Data Mining." *Knowledge and Information Systems* 14, no. 1, pp. 1–37.

[24] Taylor, J. 2007. "First Look—11Ants Analytics." Retrieved June 30, 2016, from http://jtonedm.com/2011/06/07/first-look-11ants-analytics/

[25] Caruana, R., and A. Niculescu-Mizil. 2006. "An Empirical Comparison of Supervised Learning Algorithms." In *Proceedings of the 23rd international conference on Machine learning*, pp. 161–68. New York, NY: ACM.

[26] Tibshirani, R. 1996. "Regression Shrinkage and Selection via the Lasso." *Journal of the Royal Statistical Society. Series B (Methodological)* 58, no. 1, pp. 267–88.

[27] Sayad, S. 2016a. "Model Evaluation." Retrieved June 30, 2016, from www.saedsayad.com/model_evaluation.htm

[28] Sayad, S. 2016b. "Model Evaluation-Classification." Retrieved June 30, 2016, from www.saedsayad.com/model_evaluation_c.htm

[29] Sayad, S. 2016c. "Model Evaluation-Regression." Retrieved June 30, 2016, from www.saedsayad.com/model_evaluation_r.htm

[30] Naperville [Map]. 2016. In *Google Maps*. Retrieved June 30, 2016, from www. google.com/maps/place/Naperville, IL/@41.715943,-88.2616207,11z/dat a=!4m5!3m4!1s0x880e5761e216cd07:0x87df9c2c7f203052!8m2!3d41.75 08391!4d-88.1535352!6m1!1e1

CHAPTER 5

Supply Chain Education: Are University Courses Providing the Background That Companies Want for New Employees?

Mellissa Gyimah

Introduction

The last decade of the 20th century has been particularly transient and dynamic for organizations and businesses. This is particularly seen in the supply chain management field [6]. The rate of change is increasing as we progress into the 21st century, and with that, organizations have had to be responsive to this change—and at a rapid pace! Essentially, "organizations need to be able to transform themselves to survive in the intensely competitive global environment," [6]. Part of this transformation is hiring students who have just graduated who will make brilliant employees. With these changes, it is clear that they will require unique and specific talent, in order to be competitive. But are they getting students who are academically equipped to deal with the demands of this ever-changing world? If not, why?

The Whats and the Whys of the Changes: Implications

It is important to note how the supply chain landscape is currently changing; however, not only that it is changing, this will provide us with more information in how to equip our students in the classroom, so they can succeed in the real world. The five major external forces [6] that are driving the rate of change and currently shaping the economy and political scenery are the following:

1. Globalization—Has led to a more competitively intense economic and geopolitical environment. This manifests itself in opportunities and threats—both economically and geopolitically, resulting in the volatility of supply and demand, shorter product life cycles, and blurring of traditional organizational bounds.
2. Technology—Companies have transformed their processes due to technology, and it has changed the dynamics of marketplace. We are constantly connected to one another, which has enabled individuals and small organizations to create huge opportunities for collaboration within the supply chain.
3. Organizational consolidation—After WWII product manufacturers became quite a driving force in supply chains. Retailers and their economic buying power have increased—even if they are not a large organization. Consolidation and power shift means that large retailers are given special consideration from consumer product companies. Also, mutual cost savings and better customer services are arising out of more collaboration between organizers.
4. The empowered consumer—Consumers today are more educated and empowered because of technology; they can compare prices, are given more choices and flexibility because of the many options the Internet exposes them to. This means that requirements on supply chain have greatly increased as companies are more likely to order more frequently and in smaller batches to satisfy consumers.
5. Government policy and regulation—Various levels of government (this involves federal, state, and local) have control of administrative policies and taxes, which directly affect individual businesses and supply chains. This has bred more competition and need to respond to consumer needs quickly [6].

All of these change drivers can have negative effects on organizations if they don't act accordingly, or make some changes. This helps us to understand why and how the supply chain field could be very particular in who they hire, and what skills they are looking for. It also helps to understand that it is a field where job opportunities will be salient considering its changes through the years; they need to respond to the times and the people, and that can only happen with the right work force.

Talent Search and Development

The digital supply chain, which the analyst group Gartner defines as involving a combination of the Internet of Things and advanced analytics, is rapidly transforming how businesses operate—and the type of talent they need [13]. If this is the case, trying to understand what skills are needed in the supply chain field now becomes a broader question of understanding how the supply chain field is evolving. We need to understand the past, present, and future of supply chain management in order to assess what educational values and skills students need to be equipped with to enter that space.

In general, the present looks like this: only 45 percent of supply chain executives and 40 percent of executives at U.S.-based global companies say they are extremely or very confident that their supply chain organizations have the competencies they need today, according to the 2015 supply chain survey report issued by Deloitte consulting LLP [13]. Corporate executives, however, have a far rosier view: more than three-fourths (77 percent) of the CEOs and presidents who participated in the survey said that they are extremely or very confident that the supply chain organizations have the required competencies [13]. For this third annual study, Deloitte commissioned the market research company Bayer consulting to conduct an online survey of 400 executives from U.S. companies in November 2014. Participating companies have global operations, with one or more of the following entities located outside the United States: customers operations or third-party service providers [13].

The two groups of respondents also differ sharply in their assessment of internal resources devoted to talent development. For example, more than half (54 percent) of the CEOs and presidents said that their supply chain organizations receive excellent, or very good support from the human resources development department. Only about quarter (24 percent) of all other executives said the same [13]. On average, fewer than half (45 percent) of all executives rate their employees as excellent or very good on seven leadership and professional competencies; such as strategic thinking and problem-solving, the ability to manage global or virtual teams, and ability to effectively persuade and communicate. At the same time, about two-thirds (65 percent) said that these competencies would become more important to their supply chain during the next five years, suggesting that a talent search with serious implications for companies and their customers may be developing [13].

Nevertheless, 44 percent of all executives said they expected that their companies would be able to put the necessary talent, skills, and competencies in place. That may be overly optimistic, the report suggests. Respondents to the survey, for example, reported that recruiting new talent is a greater challenge than retaining existing expertise, especially at high levels. About two-thirds of executives said that recruiting for senior director level is difficult, while less than half said that retention is difficult [13].

Universities, Coursework, and Companies

In order to better understand the implications of this endeavor, UIC will be used as a case study. UIC has been working toward aligning coursework to meet the needs of companies, while catering to student needs and trying to address the issue of soft skills versus hard skills.

The UIC Center for Supply Chain Management and Logistics (CSCML), spearheaded by Anthony Pagano, has recruited an advisory board of 12 global supply chain company leaders, providing UIC with their expertise in what they are looking for in new employees. UIC also has 14 faculty members in this group who provide students with their academic expertise and help students garner the skills they need to excel in the working world. UIC researchers noticed that despite these excellent leaders and teachers being a part of this dynamic team, there was still a gap in how student skills translated into the working world. This is particularly evident with the amount of leading companies in Chicago, which hire from universities outside of Chicago, and even Illinois. The universities of Michigan, Iowa, and Penn State are often places for companies to gain new employees, so one has to ask, what programs do they have that UIC does not, which makes students more hirable? UIC's CSCML has held many career and internship fairs and some of the feedback from companies has been that students' resumes do not have courses or topics that would be especially esteemed or valuable to companies. In many discussions with board members and faculty members, the realization was that there is a need for soft skills and hard skills in the working environment. Many of the courses offered, however, do not focus on soft skills. So, over the space of four months, faculty tried to get a better understanding of what these leaders wanted, and how it could be offered, so that students have a bigger, brighter future, and so that Illinois/Chicago companies do not have to recruit in another state.

Through this vein, the research questions became clear in order to pave the way for, (a) more courses/topics to bridge the gap between skills needed and wanted, and skills acquired, in order to (b) make students more hirable from universities with supply chain courses, such as UIC.

Research Question(s):

1. What educational background do potential employees need that will make them useful to companies hiring in the supply chain field?
2. What course/topics background do you believe would be good or are good for preparing students for a supply chain job/career?

Methodology

We adopted a mainly qualitative methodology, focused on group discussions and interviews. We also surveyed over two-dozen faculty members and supply chain global company leaders. It was clear to see that a combination of personal skills and degree qualifications were desired and seen as very salient, across the board. In fact, it was very clear that soft skills were very much desired, something that is often overlooked. Researchers also interviewed members of the Cayote team at the 33rd Annual CSCMP Chicago Roundtable Conference, and garnered information from the presentations and sessions. Overall, the field of supply chain and education has been somewhat a complex one, with many professionals recognizing that choosing the right candidate is a tenuous combination of not only educational knowledge, but also skills that may or may not be taught in the classroom. Many saw soft skills as necessary to lead teams, to build moral and to motivate. A summary of the discussion follows.

Steve Rosso—JB Hunt

With JB Hunt, I always want someone with either experience in the logistics field, or the requisite supply chain schoolwork/degree. Management degree/experience is certainly useful too. In addition to that I look for a couple other things in people. I need people who can make quick decisions, and not agonize over the smallest things. Our industry is very fast-paced, and I need people who can succeed in that. I also look for folks with strong leadership skills. In our industry, you'll be managing people from day one. You need to know how to communicate effectively, and always get the team on your side.

Ken Heller—DSCM

"We are typically looking for quantitative people. We seek degrees in Supply Chain, Engineering and IT. We have a couple of Math majors as well."

Darold Barnum (Faculty at UIC)

"I know nothing about supply chain jobs, but I do know that for almost every job in almost every field requires the ability to write well, so extra courses in English writing would be high on my list!"

Matt Liotine (Faculty at UIC)

"From what I've seen, many employers are looking for data and analytical skills, but with some grounding in operations and supply chain. Also as important, they want communication skills as well."

Ann—From Cayote (Sales)

We look for talent and someone who can and is willing to work hard; someone who can forecast and read the market—but this can be taught at our company. We don't usually see the investor side of things in my particular area, but we do need someone who can do pricing analytics. Communication is most important and absolutely key, though; to be able to give people bad news and be clear in communicating that."

—Ann also mentioned that she did not feel that her degree in Economics fully prepared her for her position, but that the company saw something in her, as well as recommendations within the company.

Joe—Cayote

The company really drew me in, because they were warm and really welcoming. I was a Behavior and Cognitive Psychology major, but at the time, the company was in a phase of hiring people with different majors and just trained them—as long as they had the talent.

Here is a simple breakdown of how skills versus academics that companies appreciated and wanted.

Skills and Topics: Breakdown

It is apparent from Figure 5.1 that companies preferred students to have skills that were personal. Many of the surveys and conversations also confirmed this. The question is, how do we draw out those personal skills within an academic framework to supplement the academic knowledge being learned, or as a supplement to the academic knowledge being acquired? The reasons for this being that even though companies were

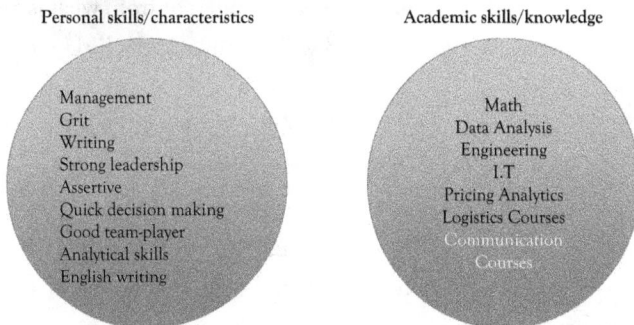

Personal skills/characteristics

Management
Grit
Writing
Strong leadership
Assertive
Quick decision making
Good team-player
Analytical skills
English writing

Academic skills/knowledge

Math
Data Analysis
Engineering
I.T
Pricing Analytics
Logistics Courses
Communication
Courses

Figure 5.1 Different types of skills

amenable to training new employees, they also mentioned how fast-paced and dynamic their fields were. Time for training is available, but they do not want to start from the basics.

It is also clear to see from these results that communication, especially, is high on the list when seeking a student to employ. But unfortunately, communication is not a course on many universities' coursework list at the present time. Collaborating with these professionals gives us a real advantage in understanding the inner workings of companies and therefore how best to equip our students to succeed. Given this information, we are now able to look into ways to incorporate a minor in communications within the supply chain management field, so that it is specific and targeted to what companies are looking for. Joseph Estrella, a lecturer in operations, supply chain management and logistics at University of Rhode Island, suggests that professionals are looking for a type of SCM certification. He has had the opportunity to discuss this at length with a range of professionals. He mentions that many of his students graduate with a certificate in Transportation and Logistics, or a certificate from the American Society of Transportation and Logistics. In addition to this, he acknowledges that technology plays a big role in supply chain management, and therefore "business professionals want students who are proficient in programs such as Excel, Access, and simulation software" [3]. His students are a prime example of how this has worked, and how they have done extremely well in the workplace, partly due to their knowledge in technology, and how they have structured their program. But he also acknowledges that one can only prepare their students so much as "the idea is that the students have to understand the concept, but how you actually use the concept is sometimes vastly different from what is taught" [3]. This is an interesting angle, and will be unpacked a little more, later on in this chapter.

While at the 33rd Annual CSCMP Chicago Roundtable Conference, Brian Gibson, a member of the Council of Supply Chain Management Professionals, discussed what companies were looking for. But he also explained that talent development is an active process—or at least, should be. He explained that the employee should be highly skilled in a key job and fits the culture—the latter is not something that can be taught. The skills he mentions that employers should be looking out for are: learning agility, synchronize functioning, broad business acumen, demand planning, risk management, and the ability to manage global issues. What he is mentioning that companies need, can only be ascertained and trained through an internship, or various student projects, so companies can see how well students perform in simulated circumstances. But he continues by saying that companies often say they need one thing, but actually hire someone with a completely different skill set. So maybe the issue is not solely on the shoulders of education and educators? This brings an important issue to the fore—the need for collaboration between universities and companies. Gibson urges companies not to just look at a student's GPA, but their ability to think critically and apply it to any given situation. Companies should look at the individual's skill set, and see where it fits in the company—if at all. If companies really are saying that they want a specific skill set, but end up hiring someone with different skills, then this make it increasingly difficult to know what they want, how to educate students, and provide students with fruitful simulated working conditions. Educators want students to feel that their knowledge and skills are wanted, needed, and put to good use. Gibson highlighted to companies the key skills they should be looking for when hiring (Figure 5.2). This in turn helps educators plan ahead. Educators know what businesses say they should look for, what they are looking for (and hopefully will not change their minds), and therefore, what educators should/can teach and offer students.

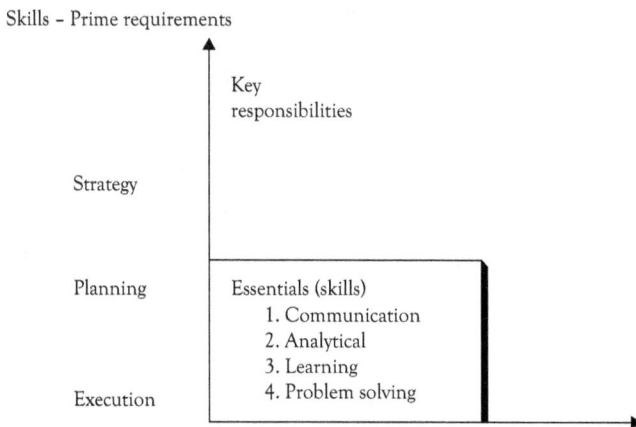

Figure 5.2 Prime skills companies should look for in an employee

Supply Chain Subjects at Universities

From this, and the many other responses and information that researchers at UIC received, they decided to compile a list of supply chain courses at universities offering supply chain as a major in the United States. We wanted to gage if supply chain courses across the board were (a) hitting some of the skills the employers said they looked for, and (b) if the list of courses/topics taught or covered some of the prime skill requirements the professor was advising companies to look for. Also, researchers were seeing a pattern emerge of soft skills versus hard skills, and needed to be able to glean how faculty could, and how faculty had been capturing/fostering the soft skills in their students. The major universities offering supply chain program laboratories were the following:

Arizona State
University of Tennessee—Knoxville
Carnegie Mellon
MIT
Texas A&M
University of Nebraska—Lincoln
Purdue
Penn State
Michigan State
Towson University
Clemson
Rutgers
University of Minnesota
University of Toronto

From this, a brief analysis was made by UIC faculty and placed into general categorization of course offering across these universities. The results were as follows:

1. Ports, Trade Agreements, Global Transportation, Channel Intermediaries
2. Types of Relationships, 3PLs, Outsourcing

3. Elements of Customer Service, Order Cycle, Improving Customer Service

4. Enterprise Resource Plannine (ERP), Radio Frequency Identification (RFID), Forecasting Techniques

5. Technology in Supply Chain

6. Materials Management and Purchasing

7. Material requirement planning (MRP), Total Quality Management (TQM), Just-in-time (JIT)

8. Service Characteristics of Modes of Transportation, Intermodal

9. Inventory Carrying Costs, Inventory Models, Uncertain Demand and Lead Times

10. Distribution Centers, Materials Handling Technology, Warehouse Layout

11. Transportation Costs and Pricing

12. Cost Modeling and Efficiency Analysis

13. System Optimization

14. e-Commerce

15. Statistical Process Control

16. Data Analytics

17. Human Resource Management

18. Strategic Planning

19. International Business

20. Labor-Management Relations

21. Negotiations

Knowing there are gaps, faculty members recognize the need to develop a curriculum for a BS Operations and Supply Chain, faculty at UIC are working to create curriculum to ensure that these gaps are addressed.

Group Discussions on Curriculum and Interest

The issue of how to encourage students to take classes has been an ongoing discussion. Going back to UIC as a case study, in March 2016, the director of UIC's Supply Chain Management Center, met with three people from the working field, and three members of faculty. Using the collated information across universities as well as within UIC, including feedback from surveys and discussions UIC researchers had garnered, a discussion ensued. It was clear that a plan of action was needed to better bridge the gap between educational needs for students to make them more marketable and ready to contribute to global companies.

Discussion 1:

Anthony—We need to discuss how we can utilize board members. We need a business plan.

Ken—That was my initial question—what is the role of the board members? Academia versus the real world—how do we go from where we are to where we want to be? Faculty teach a broad spectrum but it doesn't always translate into workplace, and it is not a quick process but what if I need someone to be on board tomorrow? Immediate business focus need, so we need a business plan. How can you create a really focused supply chain program that is really immediately applicable?

Angela—We need to get down to the basics of communication because students are using their phones and messaging but not really talking, when they should probably get on the phone.

Matt—We need some input from Board members—what courses for undergraduates and Masters programs, we need. We need core courses. Global procurement.

Jeff—Is there a supply chain intro course that is required for all students?

Angela—Operations management course is something all students have to take, so maybe we should redesign it so that supply chain is featured more to whet their appetite.

Jeff—Maybe we need to incorporate it earlier so they can make a decision about supply chain before it's too late.

Matt—We can recreate subjects we already have—that's all we can do for now. The way to really attract the students is through technology.

From this discussion, it is clear that there are many rich ideas of how to make supply chain more attractive to students, as well as what needs to be taught, and when it needs to be taught. Estrella, who was mentioned earlier, is also an expert in dialoguing about bringing the real world into the classroom. He is aware that supply chain is not a subject that a student coming out of high school would want to engage with. "What we try to do, and we have been pretty successful at it, is explain to students that supply chain is the only discipline that interacts with every other discipline in a corporation" [3]. Estrella believes that letting students know all the various topics, subjects, and issues they will be dealing with (such as procurement, inventory, marketing, advertising, and accounting), would make students more excited and willing to try supply chain—even if it is just a subject or two. But he has seen people change their majors to supply chain after taking one or two courses in the area.

There seems to be an issue with some very seminal supply chain subjects being taught a little later in the student's educational trajectory, and therefore they would have already made a decision to go into finance or engineering, because those are more well-known fields, and they know what it consists of earlier on in their education.

Discussion 2:

Angela—Are you looking for grad and undergrad courses/concentrations?

Anthony—Yes. We want an interdisciplinary minor as that's something that's missing.

Angela—Depending on the courses there may be some prerequisites . . . but minors are approx 15–18 credit hours so far.

Will—Have we looked into having field trips? It becomes real when we are on the field.

Anthony—Scheduling issues for students—it's really difficult to suit their schedules.

Ken—What if you created a one-hour class that every other week, and students spent the day at a company? I could plan a 15–20 kids to spend the day there. 3–4 visits and get credits for it, and it doesn't take away anything.

Angela—We do have a one-hour class that this is possible with. Fridays and Wednesdays are usually good for these types of visits.

Angela—Another thing I jotted down was internships. There's a boon in IDS and that's partly because students are realizing the opportunities and money available in that area. Students will get some sort of awareness and probably generate more interest.

Anthony—We spoke to the chancellor about this and he suggested we have a minor that can go across courses for internships.

Here, faculty and members are discussing ways to be more strategic in their hiring process, and the exposure students get by being a part of these companies. If exposed early enough, in conjunction with topics and courses being made available to them, possibly piquing their interest, and approach it using strategies that Estrella mentioned earlier, then they can be rerouted before they choose another academic trajectory.

Something else that is mentioned here is having an interdisciplinary minor that quickly and easily applies knowledge learned into real-life situations; and is also structured and offered in a way that enables students to maintain their busy life.

CSCML Certificate Program—What and How We Should Teach

There have been many suggestions as to what should be taught, and how it can be implemented into university curricula—starting with our own. Chris Caplice from the 33rd CSCMP Chicago Roundtable's 33rd annual conference raised another point; however, regarding the "how" of these things being taught—for optimal effect. He stated that explaining, practice, and then providing feedback, was the best way to teach face-to-face (Figure 5.3). A blended course would be most optimal for retaining information, reaching out to a wider audience, convenience of the student,

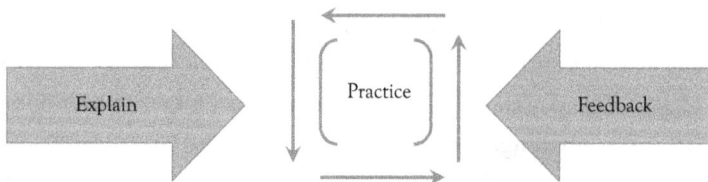

Figure 5.3 Model of how we best learn

and having them better equipped and knowledgeable about supply chain because information stays online and they can revisit it.

Caplice [4] expounded on the previous model, and suggested the following for university courses:

"Active Learning"

- Break 90-minute session into smaller chunks or modules
- Introduce and explain concept (~10–15 minutes)
- Student teams work on and submit a problem—not for grade (~10–15 minutes)
- Instructor shows solution and answers questions (~10 minutes)
- Each module is a self-contained concept with rapid feedback.

So, now, we have ideas of what needs to be taught, and how best to engage students, especially if courses will continue to be taught in person.

Devising other online programs may be farther out in the future, but at UIC, a certificate program is being developed with the purpose of efficiency and convenience. It has been designed so that it is particularly suitable for distant learners who are very busy. The certificate program aims to increase efficiency, help students to immediately apply their knowledge through simulations and student projects (which reinforces learning), develop professional leadership, and maintain busy schedules.

The program is created with the new manager in mind, and allows students to quickly understand and implement the latest concepts in supply chain management and global logistics. From procurement to forecasting, this certificate program uses real case studies and industry-wide principles that allow you to make strategic decisions to improve your company's bottom line. This interdisciplinary field pulls from transportation, information technology, marketing, industrial and civil engineering, and economics to create innovative solutions to international supply chain problems.

Table 5.1 shows a breakdown of what each week or section, or both, will look like.

1. Introduction to supply chain management: This is a two-day seminar that provides a basic understanding of logistics, the supply chain

Table 5.1 Structure of program

Introduction to supply chain management	Four seminars focusing on specialty topics	Students' present projects
Week 1 and 2	Week 3, 4, and 5	Week 6

concept, and the introductory tools necessary to work in this field. Participants registering for this seminar should be in a position where knowledge of logistics and supply chain concepts are critical to success.

2. Choose four different seminars focusing on specialty topics, including:
   - Materials Management and Purchasing
   - Lean Production and Supply Chain Management
   - Technology, Forecasting, and Decision Support
   - Transportation and Green Supply Chains
   - International Logistics
   - Manufacturing Management
   - Cost Control and Management of Logistic Activities
   - Supply Chain Network and System Management
   - Maritime Logistics
3. Final student presentations: Using tools gained throughout the series, students present their final analysis to the group and receive their certificate.

This certificate program seems like it would really bridge the gap between the working world and academia, by forging a bridge of practical understanding through the student project piece. But is what is being offered what companies are looking for?

Studies and Criticisms of Programs

A study conducted by researchers in the United States [1], focuses on the 10 universities in the United States, which have the leading undergraduate programs in supply chain management. They look at each of the university's curriculum in terms of courses and course content in order to see how each of these universities satisfies a previously established knowledge set for this field of study. They realize, very quickly, however, that there will most likely never be, in the foreseeable future, a well-structured and agreed-upon common curriculum for teaching this particular subject matter. The intended audiences are businesses that are hiring new graduates and the universities that are looking to start a similar program—so very similar to the intended audience at UIC.

The authors analyzed the course description and, if or when available, the syllabus of each of the supply chain management courses listed in the program of each of the 10 universities. They judged on which categories span over a substantial amount (15 percent or more) of the course. This was all based on the course description and the syllabus.

Based on this study and other research, common criticisms of academic program designs in comparison to practitioners' stated needs, are that the coursework usually emphasizes theoretical models that are poorly understood or very hard to apply [5]; also, academics are slow in their response to and recognition of, new approaches, or do not have the practice; therefore, their research efforts tend to be descriptive. Other studies by Visich and Khumawala [14] display a disconnect between university programs targeted at the entry level or trainee positions for undergraduates or MBAs, while practitioner studies tend to focus on upper management. Studies by Davis [7, 8], Green et al. [10], Wild [15], and Berry and Lancaster [2], all identify a dissonance between the academic preference for quantitative techniques as opposed to the practitioner preference for quantitative concepts. Additionally, employers frequently complain that graduates are lacking in softer skills—oral and written communication [11], which is what has been discussed throughout this chapter. In the Larson study [12], there was an agreement across the board that there need to be more focus on the more general managerial skills such as communication, computer skills, leadership, and relationship building, as these were seen as most important [1]. Ultimately, all these issues arose and will continue to arise because supply chain is such a new subject. The results of this study made it seem like there will never be a structured and clear way that supply chain is taught across universities. This could be problematic since it brings into question levels of qualifications and job-readiness. If all students were being taught the same, companies would know what they are getting from students, or what they need to train them on.

Conclusion

Many issues and angles have been discussed in this chapter; it has been discovered what has caused the changes in the supply chain field, how to respond to it in the workplace, and in the educational field. We have learned that soft skills are just as important, if not more (or at least there is more of it in demand) as hard skills. But ultimately, educators need to help students develop those soft skills within their curriculum to give students the best chances possible in supply chain companies when they graduate. It is clear that there are a hierarchy of skills required, and that the majority of these fall within soft skills. One will not be able to teach these students if the courses are not available, or if universities do not make themselves more marketable, however. It is not only absolutely imperative for students to have knowledge of the field, but also be able to apply it in the real world; therefore, it is important for companies and universities to collaborate. It seems that there is a need to create even more spaces and opportunities for both employer and possible employee to see if they are a fit for each other.

Brian Gibson rounded things off nicely at the Chicago Roundtable Conference with a few questions he posed and thoughts he shared. He reminds researchers, companies, and faculty that supply chain management skill sets are moving targets; that skills needed and what positions are available, need to line up. Finally, he points to the future: "How can an organization be future focused, while filling current needs for SCM talents?" [9]. This can be said of universities, too, how can universities be future-focused, while best catering to students and companies' needs?

References

[1] Bahouth, S., D. Hartmann, and G. Willis. 2014. "Supply Chain Management: How The Curricula Of The Top Ten Undergraduate Universities Meet The Practitioners' Knowledge Set." *American Journal of Business Education (Online)* 7, no. 4, p. 285.

[2] Berry, S.E., and L.M. Lancaster. 1992. "Views of Production Practitioners on the Importance of Selected POM Topics: 1978 and 1989 Practitioners Compared." *Production and Inventory Management Journal* 33, no. 2, pp. 24–31.

[3] Bradley, P. 2015. "Bringing the Real World Into the Classroom." *CSCMP's Supply Chain Quarterly*, Q2 issue: 20–22. Print.

[4] Caplice, C. 2016. "SCM Talent of the Future: An Experiment in Blended Learning." In *Proceedings of the CSCMP Chicago Roundtable's 33rd Annual Seminar*, 15 June, Embassy Suites By Hilton Chicago, Naperville, Il. Conference Presentation.

[5] Clayson, D.E., and D.A. Haley. 2005. "Marketing Models in Education: Students as Customers, Products, or Partners." *Marketing Education Review* 15, no. 1, pp. 1–10.

[6] Coyle, J.J., C.J. Langley, R.A. Novack, and B. Gibson. 2016. *Supply chain management: A Logistics Perspective*. Canada: Nelson Education.

[7] Davis, E.W. 1974. "State of the Art Survey: A Preliminary Analysis." *Production and Inventory Management Journal* 15, no. 4, pp. 1–11.

[8] Davis, E.W. 1975. "A Look at the Use of Production-Inventory Techniques: Past and Present." *Production and Inventory Management Journal* 16, no. 4, pp. 1–19.

[9] Gibson, B. 2016. "The 'Acquire' Process." In *Proceedings of the CSCMP Chicago Roundtable's 33rd Annual Seminar*, 15 June, Embassy Suites By Hilton Chicago, Naperville, Il. Conference Presentation.

[10] Green, T.B., W.B. Newsom, and S.R. Jones. 1977. "A Survey of the Application of Quantitative Techniques to Production/Operations Management in Large Corporations." *Academy of Management Journal* 20, no. 4, pp. 669–76.

[11] Hwarng, B., and C. Teo. 2001. "Translating Customers' Voices Into Operations Requirements: A QFD Application in Higher Education." *International Journal of Quality and Reliability Management* 18, no. 2, pp. 195–225.

[12] Larson, P. 2008. "Accreditation Program Design: A Survey of Supply Chain Professionals." *Journal of Enterprise Information Management* 21, no. 4, pp. 377–92.

[13] Peterson, E., and S. Klimczuk-Massion. 2015. "Corporate Leaders, Supply Chain Executives Hold Different Views on Supply Chain Talent." In *Proceedings of the CSCMP's Supply Chain Quarterly*, Q2 issue: 10–14. Print.

[14] Visich, J., and B. Khumawala. 2006. "Operations Management Curricula: Literature Review and Analysis." *Journal of Statistics and Management Systems* 9, no. 3, pp. 661–87.

[15] Wild, R. 1984. "Survey Report: The Responsibilities and Activities of UK Production Managers." *International Journal of Operations and Production Management* 4, no. 1, pp. 69–74.

CHAPTER 6

An Agent-Based Supply Chain and Freight Transportation Model: Case Study for Chicago Metropolitan Area

Zahra Pourabdollahi, Behzad Karimi, Kouros Mohammadian, and Kazuya Kawamura

Introduction

In 2011, a total of 17.6 billion tons of freight valued at $16.8 trillion were moved in the United States [1]. This is equivalent to 56.6 tons of freight worth $54,000 for each person in the United States. While the passenger vehicle use has begun to plateau in the mid-2000s, freight traffic is expected to grow considerably in the coming years. Even today, most regional transportation systems have some parts of the network that experience significant congestion due to a high volume of freight traffic. Current trends suggest that in the future, freight traffic will rival commuting trips as the leading source of congestion at many transportation links.

The remarkable increase in freight movements and their significant impacts on transportation systems, regional well-being, and economic growth, provide sufficient motivation to develop reliable analysis tools to estimate commodity flows between zones and forecast the future demand and trends of goods movements among regions. While the need to develop freight demand model to better facilitate infrastructure planning and policy development has been clearly recognized for some time *(e.g., 2 and 3)*, the current state-of-the-art practice regarding the development of behavioral freight models lags behind those of passenger travel by a considerable margin. As noted by the Strategic Highway Research Program (SHRP2) Capacity Project C20 Report [2], freight demand modeling [3] practice needs a fundamental shift, rather than incremental, short-term improvements.

This chapter outlines a behavioral agent-based supply chain and freight transportation model [3] for the Chicago Metropolitan Area. This multimodal freight model addresses critical technical and conceptual hurdles that have challenged past efforts by applying agent-based framework in which firm-level decision-making processes, including supply chain formation, are simulated at the very disaggregate level. The study tries to demonstrate the use of disaggregate, behavioral-based modeling approaches for evaluating freight policy impacts at the national/regional scale. The model will be based on sound behavioral theories to represent firm-focus level decision making in relation to commodity flows and shipment logistics.

The proposed agent-based modeling approach is unique in the focus on multiple aspects of individual firm behavior, which leads to disaggregate commodity movements, and ultimately to freight vehicle flows. The approach is analogous to the activity-based modeling approach to evaluating passenger travel demand, in that the freight goods and vehicle movements are modeled as derived demand arising from the needs and behaviors of individual firms. The proposed technology is a state-of-the-art modeling system that implements advanced behavioral-based freight modeling concepts at the disaggregate firm level.

The cutting-edge logistics choice models including mode choice, shipment size, and intermediate handling facility usage, are incorporated in the proposed framework to enhance the precision of the model in forecasting individual shipments and their attributes. Freight flows to/from intermediate facilities such as distribution centers are simulated, based on the concept of shipment chains. In addition, three-dimensional commodity-industry crosswalks for translating industry use-and-make tables into freight flow are developed to improve the accuracy of deriving industry-to-industry freight flows. Finally, the simulated freight flows are assigned to the highway network.

The rest of the chapter is structured as follows. In the second section, a brief overview of state-of-the-art freight transportation models that include explicit logistics choices is presented. In the third section, the proposed agent-based framework is introduced and the methodology and components of the framework are described. Data requirements for model development and application are discussed in the fourth section. The results of model application for the Chicago Metropolitan Area and model validation are presented in the next section. Finally, the last section presents the conclusions and the direction for future work.

Literature Review

This section provides a brief review of the state-of-the-art practice in freight forecasting and microsimulation models.

Tavasszy et al. [4] can be considered as the pioneers in developing a freight-modeling framework with logistics decisions. They developed an aggregate model that includes logistics choices, called the Strategic Model for Integrated Logistic Evaluation (SMILE) for the Netherlands. The SMILE's framework is based on a three-level chain modeling approach that includes main freight activities: production, inventory, and transportation. In another effort, Boerkamps et al. [5] developed a disaggregate commodity-based microsimulation freight transportation model, called Good TRIP, for the city of Groningen in the Netherlands. This urban freight model replicated the supply chain patterns and urban truck tours.

Good TRIP model structure was used [6] to develop a disaggregate commodity-based microsimulation model for urban freight transportation in Tokyo. Hunt et al. [7] developed a disaggregate commercial vehicle-based microsimulation for the Calgary region, using information from roughly 37,000 tours and 185,000 trips [8]. The study provided detailed information about commercial vehicle movements, including route choice, empty vehicle, and less-than-truck load treatment. Other regions in Canada (Edmonton) and the United States (Ohio) have also applied the findings of the Calgary study [9].

The Oregon Department of Transportation developed a Transportation and Land Use Model Integration Program (TLUMIP) that includes a commercial travel model component, named Statewide Integrated

Model (SWIM) [10]. SWIM is an integrated economic, land use, and transport model, in which passenger and road freight movements are integrated to simulate microlevel truck trips more effectively [11]. In a more comprehensive study, Ben-Akiva and De Jong [12] developed the aggregate–disaggregate–aggregate (ADA) freight model framework. The ADA model system is a freight transportation model that can be used at the international, national, or regional level. The ADA model system includes three distinct layers including an aggregate model that predicts production to consumption flows for zones, a disaggregate logistics model that forecasts logistics decisions such as shipment size and mode choice at the firm level, and a network model that assigns aggregate commodity flows to the traffic network.

As the review of the practical national and regional freight models revealed, the amount of attention dedicated to the freight demand forecasting has increased in recent years. However, the state-of-the-art practice in freight transportation modeling still lags behind the passenger travel demand modeling. The existing freight models usually have simple aggregate framework. Even cutting-edge of the state practice freight models have critical insufficiencies and do not completely meet the needs of public-sector freight planners, modelers, and decision makers [13, 14, 15].

Most of the current freight forecasting frameworks such as SMILE has aggregate nature or aggregate elements mainly due to the lack of disaggregate freight data. These models ignore the heterogeneity among the decision makers' behavior and shipments' attributes, which can result in a great loss of precision. These models are insensitive to the changes in logistics behavior of decision-making agents and shipments attributes. Therefore, they cannot completely capture the complexity of the decision-making process in the freight system.

Also, many of the current practical models use a vehicle-based or commodity-based four-step structure to simulate the commodity flows. Although these models have ties to the economic activities, they overlook the important role of actors and markets in the logistics system and cannot capture the behavior of actors in the markets. Moreover, many existing freight models lack explicit treatment of logistics components such as: determining the use of intermediate handling facilities, determining shipment size, or multimodal shipments at disaggregate level [16]. The drawbacks of ignoring logistics choices in freight transportation models are recognized by researchers and the field is rapidly developing in many directions, including data collection, developing advanced frameworks, and operational strategies. However, there are still significant gaps in terms of developing advanced logistics choice models for key logistics decisions and incorporating explicit logistics choice models in the freight modeling frameworks.

In summary, freight transportation modeling literature lacks appropriate agent-based microlevel models. This emphasizes on the need to develop agent-based models that incorporate supply chain relationships and logistics components in their framework to better capture the decision-making procedures. Agent-based supply chain models could better account for the complex interactions among many freight agents and markets by replicating the individual behavior of the decision makers [17] and could be integrated with passenger microsimulation models to provide a more realistic picture of the current and future traffic patterns.

Methodology and Model Framework

The proposed agent-based supply chain and freight transport model uses disaggregate behavioral-based logistics and transportation choice models to simulate commodity flows at highly disaggregate firm level [18]. The proposed model considers firms or business establishments as individual decision-making units in the freight transportation system. It assumes that logistics and supply chain decisions are made by business establishments. These logistics decisions include supplier selection, shipment size, mode choice, and shipping chain configuration. A stepwise modeling system is proposed that treats logistics decisions as discrete choice events within the simulation. The model components are described in the following.

Figure 6.1 presents the modular structure of the agent-based model. The model has a three-layered framework. In the first layer, "Economic Activity," the agents (firms) in the study area are generated, and their characteristics are determined. Several economic factors, a considerable set of data sources, and a systematic procedure is used to determine input and output values of different commodity types for these firms. The

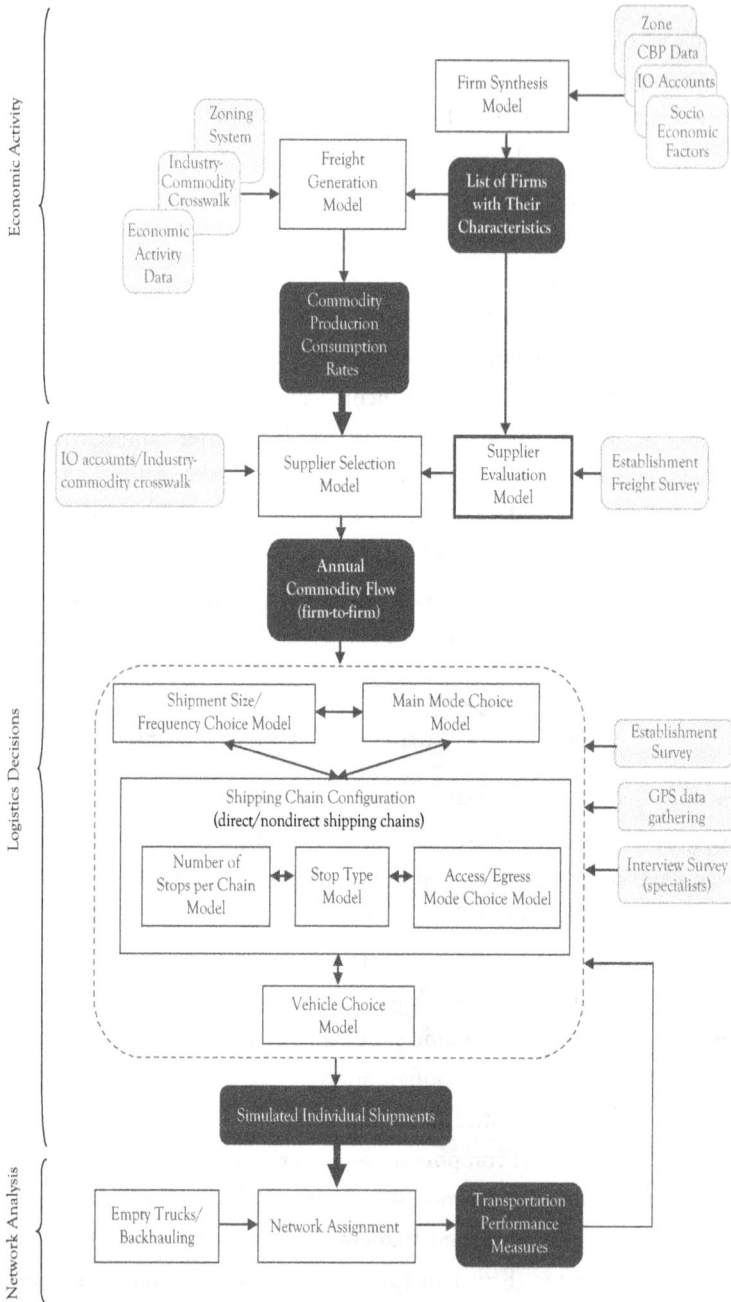

Figure 6.1 The agent-based supply chains and freight transportation model framework for the Chicago Metropolitan Area

second layer is the "Logistics Decisions" in which the logistics components of supply chains are determined in a stepwise process. First, in this layer the trade relationships between firms are formed and supplier–buyer pairs are identified using the proposed hybrid supplier selection model in this chapter. Total annual commodity flows between firms are determined using the results of supplier selection model. Next, the logistics choices including shipment size, transport mode, and shipping chain choice are determined firm-to-firm commodity flows. The final layer, "Network Analysis," deals with the assignment of commodity flows to the transportation networks, which allows further analysis and model validation.

Agents, Transported Goods, Geographical Scale

The underlying concept of this framework is the extension of the role of individual decision makers (firms) in economic activities and supply chain formation. The proposed model considers firms as the key actors in planning and execution of logistics activities in supply chains. These firms or business establishments can be supplier, shipper, or receiver of goods. There are enormous numbers of business establishments of different industry types in the United States, each of which sell or buy a considerable amount of commodities. Synthesizing all these firms and shipments is not practical due to the disaggregate data scarcity, and computational burdens in the modeling and simulation process. Therefore, some sort of aggregation is used. The concept of firm-type is proposed to be used instead of actual firms in which a firm-type represents a group of firms with the same characteristics such as industry type, employee size, and geographic location. The concept of firm-type used in the proposed model is the same as what was used in the Freight Activity Microsimulation Estimator (FAME) model. It is assumed that all firms in a firm-type group have similar behavior in the logistics decision-making process. Geographic location, employee size, and industry type of the establishments are the major characteristics that are used to synthesize firm-types. The model takes into account all commodity types that have identified value and uses the two-digit Standard Classification of Transported Goods (SCTG) system for categorizing commodities.

The framework has a very flexible structure regarding the geographical scale. It can perform analysis at nationwide scale or can be tailored to be used as a regional model. While using the framework at nation-wide scale require some aggregation in order to deal with computational issues, performing analysis at regional scale can focus on more detailed characteristics of freight movements. The proposed framework in this study covers commodity flows in the whole country; however, it mainly focuses on the freight movements in the Chicago region. A variable zoning system will be used for this purpose. The proposed zone system is comprised of township level zones in the Chicago area, counties in the areas that border Chicago region, and freight analysis framework (FAF) zones elsewhere.

Economic Activity Model

As it can be seen in Figure 6.1, the economic activity model comprises two submodels, the firm synthesis and the freight generation models. The firm synthesis model is the first model of the framework in which individual firms (agents) in the study area are generated and their major characteristics such as industry type, employee size, and geographical location will be synthesized. The synthesized firms in this step will be considered the decision-making units in the freight system and the logistics decisions will be simulated based on their behavior and characteristics.

In the freight generation submodel, the economic activity data and socioeconomic factors are used to estimate the input and output rates of different commodities for each synthesized firm. The publicly available industry input–output tables [19] and a systematic procedure are used to estimate the commodity input–output rates at the firm level. The required data for the development of this model are discussed in the next section. The methodology used for the estimation of commodity input–output rates at firm level can be divided into two steps. In the first step, a three-dimensional commodity-industry crosswalk is developed for made and used commodities by industry class. In the second step, the developed crosswalk is used to apportion aggregate input–output values between firms. Figure 6.2 summarizes the procedure for development of firm-level commodity input–output rates by industry type and employment size. These rates are then used to estimate the amount of commodities made and used by each synthesized firm.

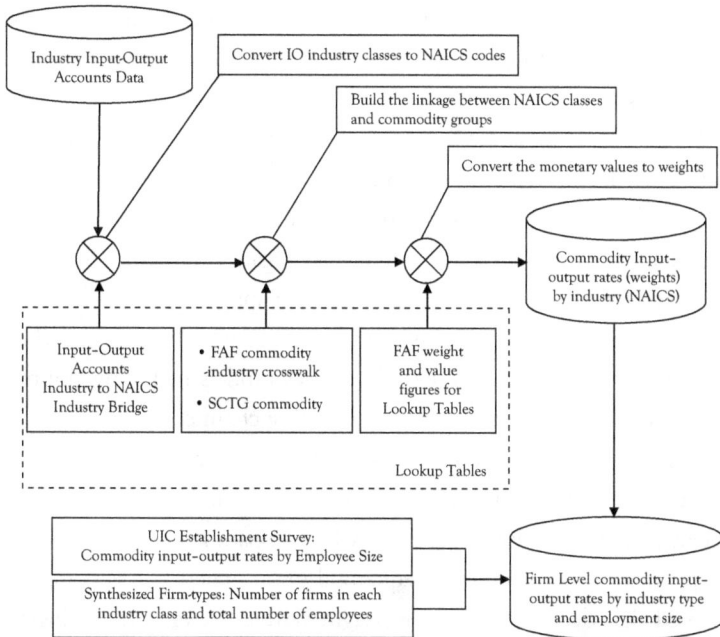

Figure 6.2 Development procedure of disaggregate commodity input–output rates

Logistics Decisions Model

The second layer of the framework is comprised of logistics submodels, which simulate the logistics choices made by individual firms in a stepwise process. The first logistics model is a hybrid supplier evaluation and selection model. The model uses a hybrid agent-based computational economic and optimization approach to capture both behavioral and economical aspects of supplier selection process for different markets. The model uses a system of ordered logit models to determine importance weights of different criteria in supplier evaluation from buyers' point of view. The estimated weights are then used to calculate a utility for each potential supplier in the market and rank them. The calculated utilities enter a mathematical programming model in which best suppliers are selected by maximizing the total accrued utility by all buyers and minimizing total shipping costs while considering the supply capacity of supplier to ensure the market clearing mechanism [20, 21]. The results of this model determine trade relationship between buyers and selected suppliers and form supply chains. It also determines the total annual amount of commodity that is traded between suppliers and buyers.

Once supply chains are built and the disaggregate annual firm-to-firm commodity flows are obtained from the supplier selection model, major logistics choices such as mode and shipment size will be determined for individual shipments. The estimated disaggregate commodity flows enter a discrete choice modeling system in which major logistics choices for these flows are determined using several submodels. The logistics choice modeling system comprises several logistics models including shipment size model, mode choice model, and shipping chain choice model.

The shipment size and mode choice are among the most critical logistics decisions. One of the major drawbacks of current freight demand models is their stepwise structure in which logistics choices are modeled independently in a simplified sequential order, whereas it is commonly accepted that decision makers in freight systems determine the logistics choices for each shipment simultaneously. Review of literature showed that mode choice and shipment size are highly correlated logistics decisions and should be modeled simultaneously [22]. To address this, a joint copula-based model [23] is employed to determine mode and shipment size choices simultaneously. It is assumed that the joint model can take into account the effects of common causal factors and can better capture the effects of each choice on another one. Therefore, it will provide more precise results.

In the next submodel, for each shipment, the shipping chain configuration is determined. Shipping chain configuration is a key logistics choice that has been ignored or treated insufficiently in current freight transportation models. A shipping chain is defined as the physical connection between supplier and buyer of goods or origin and destination of the shipment [24]. A *shipping chain* can be a combination of one or more links depending on the number of stops per shipping chain. Based on the number and type of stops used for each shipment, different shipping chain categories can be defined.

In this study, a system of decision-tree models is employed to determine the *shipping chain* configuration of shipments by identifying the number and type of intermediate stops (consolidation center, distribution center, intermodal terminal) in the supply chain [24]. The proposed decision-tree models are developed using 80 percent of the observations in the data and the remaining 20 percent are used to validate the models. The results of model estimation indicated that shipments' attributes are the most significant variables in predicting the configuration of shipping chain.

Network Analysis Model

The final layer of the proposed framework is the network analysis model, which takes the disaggregate shipments with specified characteristics derived from previous layers as input and assign them to the relevant networks. In this layer, first, a procedure is used to convert disaggregated commodity flows to vehicle trips and generates truck on demand (OD) tables before assigning the flows to the network. This is an essential procedure to convert tons of commodities to truck trips and prepare the input for the traffic assignment and network analysis. Variety of vehicle sizes and the fact that a significant portion of vehicles might be empty or partially loaded, make this task extremely challenging. In this study, only the simulated truck flows are converted to truck trips and assigned to the network.

The conversion process used in this study is similar to the FAF procedure to transform commodity tonnage to truck payload [25]. In this procedure, first, commodity volumes (tonnage) are allocated between five primary truck configurations. Then, commodity-based truck equivalency factors are used to convert tonnage to truck trips for all truck classes. Finally, the percentage of empty trucks for each truck class is estimated using the empty truck factors from FAF model. The estimated truck OD tables are then assigned to the highway network. The assignment of shipments to the networks provides valuable inputs for further analyses; particularly, it produces performance measures for impact and policy analysis.

Data Needs for Development and Application

As with any agent-based model, development of the proposed agent-based supply chain model requires detailed and comprehensive data including information on decision-makers' processes, individual shipments' attributes, and spatial information on economic activities in the study area. As mentioned earlier, the objective of the proposed model is to put forward a disaggregate agent-based microlevel framework for freight transportation that includes major logistics choices, while keeping the dimensionality and complexity of the model manageable and the need for the survey and private input data the least. Ideally, we try to utilize the publicly available freight data for the development of the models such as Industry Input–Output Accounts [19], County Business Patterns [26], Commodity Flow Survey (CFS) [27], and FAF [28]. However, since the publicly available data does not capture the necessary disaggregate information, we relied on the provided data from the University of Illinois at Chicago (UIC) freight establishment survey [29] for the estimation of the disaggregate logistics models in the second layer of the framework.

The survey has been carried out at UIC [29] to shed light on the logistics decision-making behaviors at firm level. The survey aimed for shipping managers at the respondent business establishments as the survey participants gathered information about the shipments attributes and logistics choices from these respondents. The survey was conducted online and included three major parts. First part asked about the relevant characteristics of the establishment including location, employee size, total annual shipments, major suppliers and supply chains, and so on. The second section of the survey gathered information about five most recent shipments at firm including origin, destination, mode of transportation, commodity type, value and weight of the shipment, shipping chain configuration, and so on. The last part of the survey involved optional contact information with a set of evaluation questions about the survey. The survey provided information on more than 1,850 shipments from 973 business establishments.

Model Application

The agent-based model was employed to simulate disaggregate supply chains in the United States. However, as mentioned earlier, it mainly focuses on the goods movement in the Chicago Metropolitan Area. This section summarizes some of the model application and validation results.

The first component of the agent-based model, economic activity model, synthesized business establishments in the study area. There are more than 7.6 million business establishments in the United States [26]. The firm synthesis model uses 333 zones in the zoning system, 87 industry classes, and 7 employee size groups to categorize these business establishments. Using the firm synthesis model, these business establishments are categorized into 70,116 firm-type groups that are considered as the agents in the simulation process.

As explained earlier, a multistep procedure is used to estimate the commodities production and consumption (input–output) values for synthesized firms. Table 6.1 presents the total estimated input and output values for 14 classes of commodities and compares them with the reported values in FAF data. As the table shows, the total estimated production and consumption values are pretty close to the reported values in FAF data, except for "Agricultural and Forestry Products." The significant difference between estimated and reported values for "Agricultural and Forestry Products" is mainly due to the absence of economic data on firms in the "Crop Production" and "Animal Production" industries in the County Business Patterns datasets. These industries are excluded from this study and no firm-type of these industry classes are generated in the simulation process.

In total, more than 13.4 billion tons of made commodities worth more than $10.6 million and more than 13.7 billion tons of used commodities worth more than $10.7 million are assigned to firms in the freight generation model. As the table shows, the slim difference between FAF and estimated input–output values at aggregate scale confirms that the developed crosswalks and input–output rates can accurately distribute made and used values between firms. The small differences between FAF and estimated values are due to data insufficiency and missing values in development of the crosswalks and input–output rates.

Figure 6.3 depicts the estimated production and consumption values for "Paper Products" to provide an example of the output of the economic activity model and compares the estimated values with FAF data. The presented values in the figure are firm level made and used values that have been aggregated to zone level.

Since the results cannot be clearly presented in figures for the Illinois state due to small zone system, Table 6.2 is developed to compare aggregated values for Illinois.

Table 6.1 Total estimated and FAF production and consumption values (KTON)

Commodity class	FAF production consumption	Estimated production	% Difference production	Estimated consumption	% Difference consumption
Agriculture and forestry products	2,842,869	2,017,092	29.00%	2,447,513	13.90%
Products of mining	4,371,775	4,365,197	0.20%	4,265,851	2.40%
Petroleum products	1,448,457	1,406,551	2.90%	1,389,943	4.00%
Chemical and pharmaceutical products	670,304	669,552	0.10%	639,476	4.60%
Wood products	875,363	868,342	0.80%	865,240	1.20%
Paper products	265,028	263,942	0.40%	263,275	0.70%
Nonmetallic mineral products	1,316,807	1,313,754	0.20%	1,311,939	0.40%
Metal and machinery products	679,572	677,783	0.30%	657,884	3.20%
Electronic, electrical, and precision equipment	60,107	60,099	0.00%	59,796	0.50%
Motorized and transportation vehicles and equipment	141,682	141,612	0.00%	139,001	1.90%
Household and office furniture	35,406	35,406	0.00%	35,400	0.00%
Plastic, rubber, and miscellaneous Manufactured products	274,305	273,952	0.10%	271,861	0.90%
Textiles and leather products	51,625	51,474	0.30%	51,202	0.80%
Waste and scrap	1,276,473	1,273,808	0.20%	1,267,943	0.70%

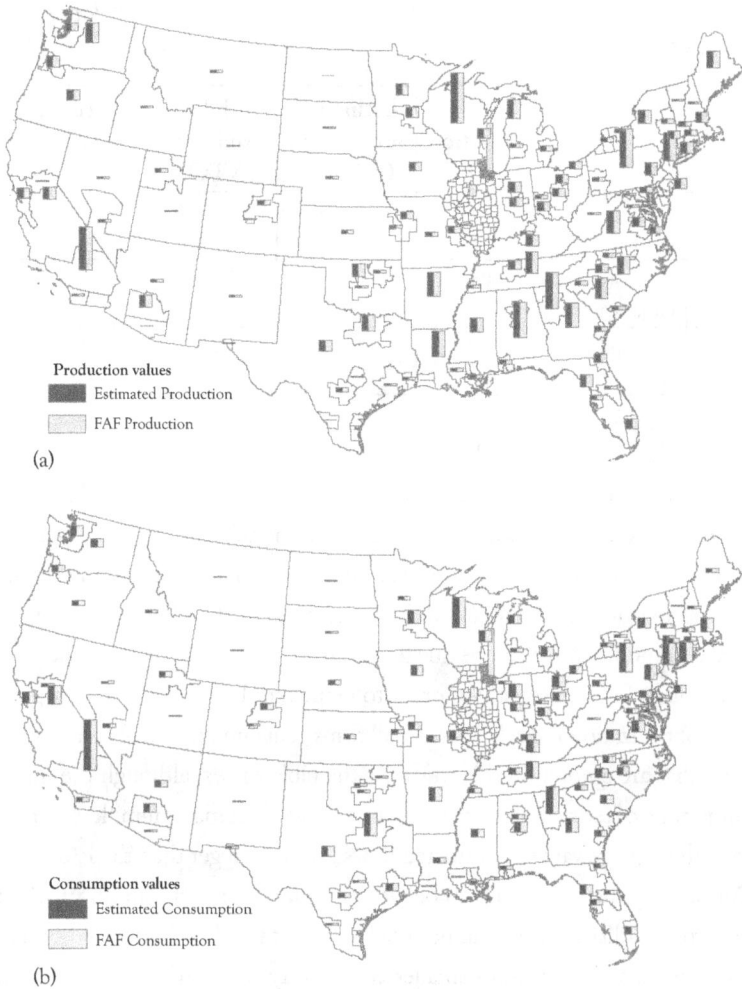

Figure 6.3 *Comparison of estimated and FAF made (a) and used (b) values for "Paper Products"*

In the next module, supplier–buyer pairs are identified and supply chains are replicated using the behavioral hybrid supplier evaluation and selection. The proposed agent-based model forms supply chains for 14 types of commodities (markets) and estimates total annual commodity flows at firm-to-firm level. Based on the results of the freight generation model, 621,325 buyers have to be connected to a set of 99,986 potential suppliers. Table 6.3 presents the total estimated commodity flows for different markets (classes of commodities) and compares them with the FAF

Table 6.2 Estimated and FAF production-consumption of "Paper Products" in Illinois

FAF zone	Definition	FAF production (KTON)	Estimated production (KTON)	FAF production (KTON)	Estimated production (KTON)
171	Chicago mega-region	12,086	12,038	13,807	13,752
172	St. Louis mega-region	305	304	344	340
179	Remainder of Illinois	2,861	2,850	3,851	3,816

commodity flows. It should be noted that the estimated firm-level flows are aggregated to the FAF zone level, so they can be compared with FAF flows.

As the table shows, the supplier selection model simulates 85.1 percent (around 12 billion tons) of 2007 FAF domestic commodity flows that are transported by truck, rail, air, and courier modes. This difference between total commodity flows can be due to the exclusion of very small supplier and buyer firms from this study in order to reduce the computational complexity of optimization model. These small firms generate very small commodity flows that are ignored in this study. As the table shows, although the maximum value of estimated flows are much smaller than maximum flow in FAF data, the average value of estimated flows is much bigger than the FAF data. Considering the huge intervals between minimum and maximum values of FAF commodity flows, it can be concluded that the distribution of flows in FAF data is skewed toward smaller commodity flows, while the proposed model simulates more homogenously distributed commodity flows.

Figure 6.4 shows the replicated supply chains for "Electronics, Electrical, and Precision Equipment" market as an instance of the output of supplier selection model for the Illinois state. It compares the modeled supply chains with FAF commodity flow patterns. It should be noted that the firm-level commodity flows are aggregated to the zone-level flows for this presentation.

As the figure shows, the simulated supply chains are different from the FAF commodity flow patterns. Although the commodity flow ranges are similar, the distribution of flows within this range is completely different. While there are more small size (KTON) flows presented in FAF data,

Table 6.3 Total FAF and estimated commodity flows for all classes of commodities

Commodity class (market)	FAF flows (KTON)				Estimated flows (KTON)			
	Total	Min	Max	Mean	Total	Min	Max	Mean
Agriculture and forestry products	2,842,869	0.001	165,059	245	2,017,092	1.07	98,033	3,565
Products of mining	4,371,775	0.001	96,643	551	3,788,499	1.04	106,852	6,051
Petroleum products	1,448,457	0.001	69,445	217	1,229,671	0.05	22,832	2,231
Chemical and pharmaceutical products	668,304	0.001	76,502	57	498,310	0.02	13,217	592
Wood products	875,363	0.001	76,502	105	775,975	0.002	16,761	1,363
Paper products	265,028	0.001	7,515	24	187,974	0.77	1,986	205
Nonmetallic mineral products	1,316,807	0.001	55,543	137	1,151,567	9.06	23,697	1,771
Metal and machinery products	679,572	0.001	15,697	52	577,992	0.14	6,385	395
Electronic, electrical, and precision equipment	60,107	0.001	2,294	4	43,054	0.06	1,218	26
Motorized and transportation Vehicles and equipment	141,682	0.001	5,793	15	122,828	0.1	2,198	139
Household and office furniture	35,406	0.001	1,140	3	31,352	0.22	222	23
Plastic, rubber, and miscellaneous manufactured products	274,305	0.001	9,915	21	210,286	0.01	2,961	164
Textiles and leather products	51,625	0.001	4,341	5	45,562	0.02	951	37
Waste and scrap	1,276,473	0.001	59,798	145	1,118,231	2.19	16,658	2,803
Total	14,307,773	0.001	165,059	70.9	11,798,393	0.01	106852	929.0

Simulated flows (KTON)
  1.15 - 37.24
  37.25 - 104.03
  104.04 - 258.50
  258.51 - 537.17

(a)

FAF flows (KTON)
  0.99 - 13.25
  13.26 - 45.41
  45.42 - 142.12
  142.13 - 459.51

(b)

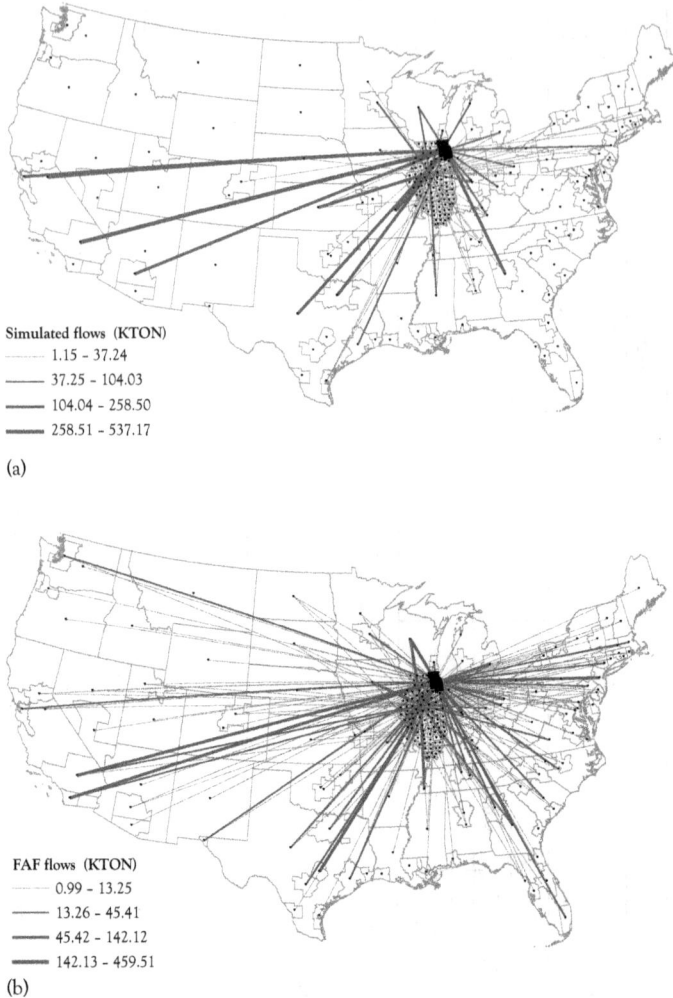

Figure 6.4 Simulated and FAF flows for "Electronic, Electrical, and Precision Equipment" market (a) Simulated flows (b) FAF flows

the simulated commodity flows in this study are more evenly distributed by size (KTON). This difference can be due to the exclusion of small production and consumption values from this study. These small production and consumption values generate small size commodity flows. However, since they are excluded from this study, small size commodity flows are underestimated. Also, this study uses a behavioral optimization supply chain model to simulate commodity flows while the FAF model employs

Table 6.4 Modal splits based on weight of transported commodities

Mode	Proposed model	CFS 2007	FAF
Truck	82.9%	82.22%	82.58%
Rail	11.4%	17.43%	13.03%
Air	2.0%	0.03%	0.08%
Courier	3.7%	0.32%	4.32%

a data mining–based flow matrix construction technique [30] to estimate commodity flows. The different approaches used for estimation of commodity flows in the two models can be another source of dissimilarities between FAF and simulated commodity flows in this study. The same analysis was performed for other 13 markets, which resulted in similar outcome and conclusion.

The copula-based joint mode choice and shipment size model is used to simulate mode of transportation and shipment size of the simulated commodity flows between firms. Four modes of transportation including truck, rail, air, and courier and five discrete shipment size classes including (0–200 lbs), (201–1,000 lbs), (1,001–4,000 lbs), (4,000–30,000 lbs), and (more than 30,000 lbs) are considered in the model and simulated in this study. The FAF [28] and CFS data are used to compare modal split. Table 6.4 presents estimated modal split and compare them with reported values in FAF and CFS data. It should be noted that the 2007 CFS [27] was used to calibrate the copula-based mode choice model.

Summary and Conclusion

The objective of the proposed model was to put forward an agent-based microlevel supply chain and freight transport model that includes major logistics choices, while keeping the dimensionality and complexity of the model manageable, and the need for the survey and private input data the least. The proposed state-of-the-art microsimulation model provides a platform to test how various policy measures and major infrastructure investments can alleviate the negative impacts of freight transportation and how implementing efficient policies would make the freight transportation system more sustainable. It provides a sophisticated simulation tested system that allows decision makers to quantify economical, social, and environmental benefits and costs of different freight transportation strategies.

In addition, the approaches used to develop individual components of the proposed model, for example, freight generation, supplier selection, logistics choices, and multimodal network analysis, can be adopted to improve the existing tools such as FAF. It is expected that the disaggregate construct of the model makes it possible to feed the output of this national model to various regional freight models.

The model addresses key research issues including but not limited to:

- The lack of microlevel freight analysis tools.
- Low level of detail in commodity-industry crosswalks.
- Highly aggregated commodity input–output tables.
- A lack of information about behavioral supplier evaluation and selection process.
- The lack of disaggregate logistics choice models.
- Little consideration for multimodal disaggregate freight movements.
- The need for development of microlevel network analysis tool for freight movements.

References

[1] U.S. Department of Transportation. 2013. Freight Facts and Figures 2013. Report to the Federal Highway Administration: Office of Freight Management and Operations.

[2] Chase, K.M., P. Anater, and T. Phelan. 2013. *SHRP 2 Report* S2-C20-RR1: *Freight Demand Modeling and Data Improvement*. Washington, D.C: Transportation Research Board of the National Academies.

[3] Comi, A., P. Delle Site, F. Filippi, and A. Nuzzolo. 2012. "Urban Freight Transport Demand Modelling: A State of the Art." *European Transport* 51.

[4] Tavasszy, L.A., B. Smeenk, and C.J. Ruijgrok. 1998. "A DSS for Modeling Logistics Chains in Freight Transport Policy Analysis." In *International Transactions in Operational Research* 5, no. 6, pp. 447–59.

[5] Boerkamps, J., A. van Binsbergen, and P. Bovy. 2000. "Modeling Behavioral Aspects of Urban Freight Movement in Supply Chains." In *Transportation Research Record* 1725, pp. 17–25.

[6] Wisetjindawat, W., and K. Sano. 2003. "A Behavioral Modeling in Micro-Simulation for Urban Freight Transportation." In *Journal of the Eastern Asia Society for Transportation Studies* 5, pp. 2193–208.

[7] Hunt, J., K. Stefan, and A. Brownlee. 2006. "Establishment-Based Survey of Urban Commercial Vehicle Movements in Alberta, Canada: Survey Design, Implementation, and Results." In *Transportation Research Record* 1957, pp. 75–83.

[8] Stefan, K., J. McMillan, and J. Hunt. 2005. "Urban Commercial Vehicle Movement Model for Calgary, Alberta, Canada." In *Transportation Research Record* 1921, pp. 1–10.

[9] Yang, C.H., J.Y.J. Chow, and A. Regan. 2009. "State-of-the Art of Freight Forecasting Modeling: Lessons Learned and the Road Ahead." In *Proceedings of the 88th Annual Meeting of the Transportation Research Board*, January 11–15. Washington DC.

[10] Donnelly, R. 2007. "A Hybrid Microsimulation Model of Freight Flows." In *Proceedings of the 4th International Conference on City Logistics*, July 11–13. eds. E. Taniguchi and R.G. Thompson. pp. 235–46. Crete, Greece: Institute for City Logistics.

[11] Hunt, J.D., R. Donnelly, J.E. Abraham, C. Batten, J. Freedman, J. Hicks, P.J. Costinett, and W.J. Upton. 2001. "Design of a Statewide Land Use Transport Interaction Model for Oregon." In *Proceedings of World Conference on Transportation Research*, p. 19. Seoul, South Korea.

[12] Ben-Akiva, M., and G. de Jong. 2008. "The Aggregate-Disaggregate-Aggregate (ADA) Freight Model System." In *Recent Developments in Transport Modelling: Lessons for the Freight Sector*, eds. M.E. Ben-Akiva, H. Meersman and E. van de Voorde. pp. 117–34. Australia: Emerald press.

[13] Liedtke, G., and H. Schepperle. 2004. "Segmentation of the Transportation Market with Regard to Activity-Based Freight Transport Modelling." *International Journal of Logistics Research and Applications* 7, no. 3, pp. 199–218.

[14] Hesse, M., J.P. Rodrigue. 2004. "The Transport Geography of Logistics and Freight Distribution." *Journal of Transportation Geography* 12, no. 3, pp. 171–84.

[15] Friesz, T.L., J. Holguín-Veras. 2005. "Dynamic Game-Theoretic Models of Urban Freight: Formulation and Solution Approach." In *Methods and Models in Transport and Telecommunications, Advances in Spatial Science*, pp. 143–61. Berlin: Springer.

[16] De Jong, G., and M. Ben-Akiva. 2007. "A Micro-Simulation Model of Shipment Size and Transport Chain Choice." In *Transportation Research Part B: Methodological* 41, no. 9, pp. 950–65.

[17] Wisetjindawat, W., K. Sano, S. Matsumoto, and P. Raothanachonkun. 2007. "Microsimulation Model for Modeling Freight Agents Interactions

in Urban Freight Movement." In *Proceedings of 86th Annual Meeting of the Transportation Research Board*, January 21–25. Washington DC.

[18] Pourabdollahi, Z. 2015. An Agent-based Freight Transportation Modeling Framework [PhD dissertation]. University of Illinois, Chicago.

[19] Bureau of Economic Analysis. 2014. Industry Economic Accounts, Input-Output Accounts, U.S. Department of Commerce. www.bea.gov/industry/index.htm#benchmark_io (accessed April 2014).

[20] Pourabdollahi, Z., B. Karimi, and K. Mohammadian. 2014. "A Multi-Criteria Supplier Evaluation Model in a Supply Chain." *Submitted to the 93rd Annual Meeting of the Transportation Research Board*, Washington, D.C.

[21] Pourabdollahi, Z., B. Karimi, K. Mohammadian, and K. Kawamura. 2016. "(Submitted for Review) A Hybrid Agent-based Computational Economics and Optimization Approach For Supplier Selection Problem." *Submitted to the 95th Annual Meeting of the Transportation Research Board*, Washington, D.C.

[22] Windisch, E., G.C. De Jong, R. van Nes, and S.P. Hoogendoom. 2010. "A Disaggregate Freight Transport Model of Transport Chain and Shipment Size Choice." In *Proceedings of European Transport Conference*, October 11–13. Glasgow, Scotland.

[23] Pourabdollahi, Z., B. Karimi, and A. Mohammadian. 2013. "A Joint Model of Freight Mode and Shipment Size Choice." *Transportation Research Records: Journal of the Transportation Research Board* 2378, pp. 84–91. Washington D.C.

[24] Pourabdollahi, Z., B. Karimi, A. Mohammadian, and K. Kawamura. 2014. "Shipping Chain Choices in Long Distance Supply Chains: Descriptive Analysis and a Decision Tree Model." *Transportation Research Records: Journal of the Transportation Research Board* 2410, pp. 58–66. Washington D.C.

[25] Oak Ridge National Lab. 2011a. FAF3 Freight Traffic Analysis, Submitted by Battelle.

[26] U.S. Census Bureau. 2014. County Businesses Patterns (CBP-2007). www.census.gov/programs-surveys/cbp.html (accessed April 2014).

[27] U.S. Census Bureau. 2014. Commodity Flow Survey (CFS-2007), U.S. Department of Commerce, www.census.gov/econ/cfs/ (accessed April 2014).

[28] U.S. Department of Transportation. 2014. Freight Analysis Framework (FAF3), Federal Highway Administration: Office of Operations. www.ops.fhwa.dot.gov/freight/freight_analysis/faf/ (accessed April 2014).

[29] Sturm, K., Z. Pourabdollahi, and A. Mohammadian. 2013. "Descriptive and Non-Response Bias Analyses for a Nationwide Freight Establishment Survey." In *The 92nd Annual Meeting of the Transportation Research Board*, Washington, D.C.

[30] Oak Ridge National Lab. 2011b. The Freight Analysis Framework Version 3 (FAF3): A Description of the FAF3 Regional Database And How It Is Constructed, U.S. Department of Transportation.

CHAPTER 7

Kaplan–Meier Estimators for Single Product Demand Using Inventory Level Time-Series

J. Christopher Westland

Demand Forecasts in Supply-Chain Optimization

Effective transportation system and supply chain design is predicated on the availability of accurate inputs to the modeling process. Arguably, the most important of these is a forecast of consumer demands for a product or service. Forecasts of product demand determine how much inventory is needed, how much product to make, and how much material to purchase from suppliers to meet forecasted customer needs. This in turn determines the kind of transportation that will be needed and where plants, warehouses, and distribution centers will be located so that products and services can be delivered on time. Without accurate forecasts large stocks of costly inventory must be kept at each stage of the supply chain to compensate for the uncertainties of customer demand. If there are insufficient inventories, customer service suffers because of late deliveries and stock-outs.

The current chapter addresses the research question of how you create an accurate customer demand forecast for a single item inventory where demand is indirectly observed by tracking inventory levels. Inventory management and control are often myopic. The only information that management has available for the customer demand input to their policy model comes from the inventory levels over time, which is inherently right-censored by stock-outs (where demand exceeds supply). At best, such indirect measures of demand are often independently entered into the inventory management optimization algorithms, which management relies on to minimize the combined holding, logistics, stock-out, insurance, and risk management, and obsolescence costs. But too often demand estimators are generated as a part of an optimization algorithm. This can be problematic because demand forecasts are primarily statistical inference endeavors. They should ideally be separated from the policy implementations of supply chain optimization, which are primarily mathematical programming problems.

Most supply chain optimization algorithms attempt to construct such forecasts organically as a dynamic process embraced within their algorithm; this yields both suboptimal forecasts, as well as suboptimal inventory management policy implementation. The need for tractability in such models forces simplifications that can significantly degrade performance and introduce bullwhip and related synchronization problems into the various subprocesses that comprise the supply chain [1, 2]. Boyle et al. [3] presented findings from electronics industry, where original equipment manufacturers suffered significant inventory carrying costs because they could not predict demand beyond a four-week horizon. Moon et al. [4] provide a case study of improvements in demand forecasting Alcatel-Lucent, which achieved nearly 80 percent reduction in inventory. Reyes et al. [5] and Reyes and Frazier [6] argued that poor demand forecasting in an era of increasing demand information but many companies at a competitive disadvantage; Zhao et al. [7, 8], Bayraktar et al. [9], and Wright and Yuan [10] offered methods and tools that enabled improvements in supply chain management through better integration of demand. Albertson and Aylen [11] explored autoregressive models for demand in supply chain management; Chatfield and Yar [12] suggested that many of these models oversimplified demand behavior. The body of prior research in customer demand elicitation in standard supply chain optimization problems suggests that suboptimal demand forecasting is a significant problem.

The remainder of the chapter delineates a methodology to address customer demand forecast errors that can contribute to suboptimization in supply chain algorithms. It introduces a separable demand forecasting based on Kaplan–Meier estimators using data only from inventory levels (in the second section); provides examples of the application of such estimators to elicit demand forecast time-series, as well as comparative static price–quantity demand functions (in the third section); and incorporates the forecasts generated from Kaplan–Meier estimators using data only from inventory levels into a basic inventory restocking algorithm (in the fourth section).

Kaplan–Meier Estimators for Single Product Demand Using Restocking Information

Huh et al. [13] addressed the problem of forecasting demand with censored data in the context of a classic supply chain problem called the "Newsvendor Problem." The model is a mathematical model in operations management and applied economics used to determine optimal inventory levels characterized by fixed prices and uncertain demand for a perishable product, with censoring of demand $\tilde{D}$ empirical data when demand exceeds inventory level q. It was first presented in a financial context in Edgeworth [14] and reappeared in Arrow and Harris [15] in an OR context. The more general problem has been addressed in Samartzis [16].

The standard newsvendor profit function is $profit = E_{\tilde{D}}\left(p \times min \left[q, \tilde{D} \right] \right) - cq$ where p and c are fixed sales and acquisition values per unit. The profit maximizing stocking quantity of the newsvendor, which maximizes expected profit is $q = F^{-1}\left(\dfrac{p-c}{p} \right)$ were $F^{-1}(.)$ is the quantile function of the demand random variable (this is called Littlewood's rule).

Assume a time-series of observations on an underlying independent and identically exponentially distributed sequence of time periods between software acquisitions by manufacturing firms $\{\ldots\ t_l,\ \ldots\ t_j,\ \ldots\}$, which is potentially left- and right-censored at $[t_l,\ t_r]$ (Figure 7.1).

The Kaplan–Meier estimator is a nonparametric statistic [19, 23] used to estimate the survival function $S(t) = P(T > t) = \int_t^\infty f(u)\,du - 1 - F(T)$ from lifetime data, typically in medical studies to measure the fraction of patients living for a certain amount of time after treatment. It can take

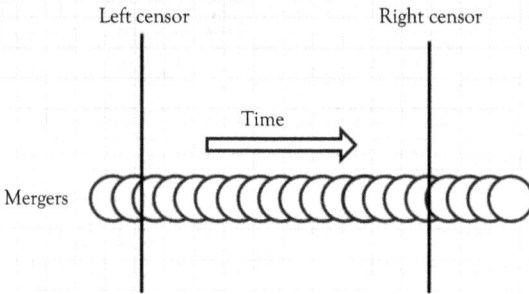

Figure 7.1 Restocking time-series (conceptual)

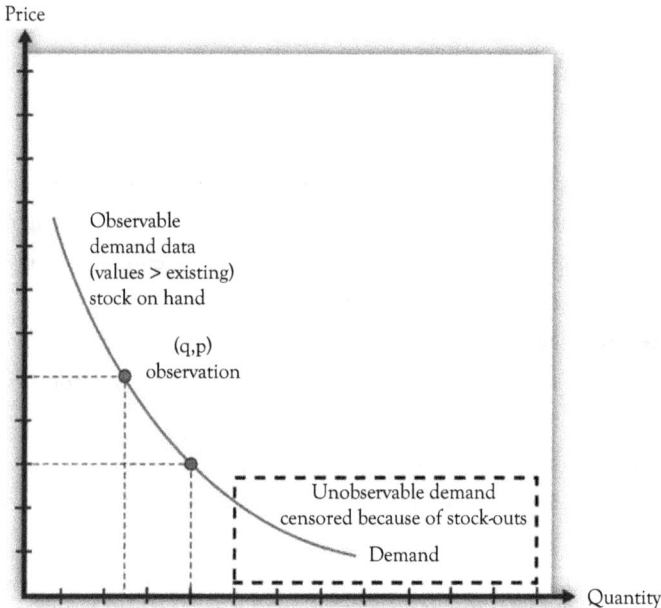

Figure 7.2 Demand curve censored by stock-outs

into account right-censoring, which occurs if a patient withdraws from a study, is lost to follow-up, or is alive without event occurrence at last follow-up. When no censoring occurs, the Kaplan–Meier curve is one minus the empirical distribution function (Figure 7.2).

In demand estimation from inventory stocking levels, right-censoring occurs because once we stock-out of a product, we are prevented from eliciting information on actual demand.

Assume that we acquire a dataset of n observations $\{(p_i, q_i)\}$ with a common distribution function $F(q) = P(q_i < q)$. Let $\{S_i\}$ be a sequence of independent random variables indicating remaining inventory stock, which are independent of $\{(p_i, q_i)\}$. Suppose that the (p_i, q_i) are not completely observable (are censored) and that observations are $(q_i, \delta_i), i = 1, ..., n$ where

$$\tilde{q}_i = q_i \wedge \delta_i \text{ where } \delta_i = I_{\{q_i \wedge \delta_i\}^*}$$

where $\wedge$ is the right-censoring maximum, and δ_i is the censorship indicator. The Kaplan–Meier estimator $\tilde{F}_n$ is

$$1 - \tilde{F}_n(s) = \prod_{s \leq t} \left(1 - \frac{\Delta N_n(s)}{Y_n(s)}\right)$$

where $0/0 = 0$, $\Delta N_n(s) = N_n(s) - \Delta N_n(s-)$ and

$$N_n(s) = \#\{i \leq n : \tilde{q}_i \leq s, \delta_i = 1\}$$

$$Y_n(s) = \#\{i \leq n : \tilde{q}_i > s\} = \sum_{i=1}^{n} I_{\{q_i \wedge \delta_i \geq s\}}$$

where #(*condition*) is the count of items satisfying the condition. Gill [17] established the uniform consistency and functional central limit theorem of $\tilde{F}_n$ under considerably weaker assumptions than previous research.

Figure 7.3 assumes a fixed restocking policy that increments inventory V by units every w time periods. This policy will later be expanded to include functions of the demand variable, $\tilde{V} = f(\tilde{D})$ and $\tilde{w} = g(\tilde{D})$, but we will start with a naïve restocking policy, depicted in Figure 7.3. In the naïve policy case, inventory change in period w is $\Delta \tilde{X}(w) = \tilde{D}(w) + V \Rightarrow \tilde{D}(w) = \Delta \tilde{X}(w) - V$. So the only sample needed

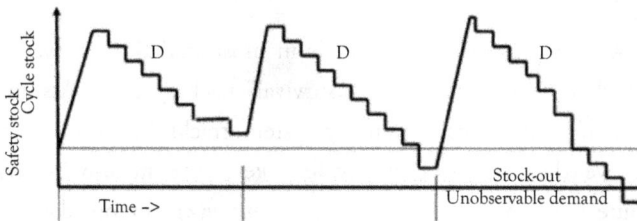

Figure 7.3 *Quantity demand over time, with fixed restocking policy*

for estimation is the time-series of orders but since the censoring occurs because of stock-outs, the estimation needs to be done with the transformed $\Delta \widetilde{X}(w)$ random variable.

We can use this model to compute two unique, identified cumulative distribution functions $\widetilde{F}_n(p) = \widetilde{G}_n(q)$. Since both the demand curve and the cumulative distribution function are unique and identified (by the standard assumption that demand is not time-varying) then for any (p, q) sampled from the real-world demand curve we will have $\widetilde{F}_n(p) = \widetilde{G}_n(q)$. This implies that we can use the quantiles to sweep out the demand curve. For any quantile x you have a particular demand and price

$$\left(p, q\right)_x = \left(\widetilde{F}_n^{-1}(x), \widetilde{G}_n^{-1}(x)\right)$$

where x can be considered a distance from the zero probability price/quantity pair, and parametrically sweeps out the demand curve as it increases toward 1. This "empirical" demand curve may be denoted as $q = \widetilde{D}(p)$.

Once we have a demand curve $q = D(p)$ that defines the one-dimensional path from which all $\{p, q\}$ observations are drawn, we can add some machinery to keep our analysis on the curve. For example, with integration define the scalar field $D : U \subseteq \mathbb{R}^2$ then the path integral along a piecewise smooth demand curve $C \subset U$ is:

$$\int_c D \, dp = \int_a^b D\big(p(t)\big) \frac{dp(t)}{dt} dt \ where \ (a, b) \ are$$
$$probability \ (0,1) \ bounds \ on \ the \ sampled \ prices$$

This converts an ostensibly two-dimensional time-series of $\{p, q\}$ observations into an equivalent one-dimensional time-series of observations.

Kaplan–Meier Estimation Example with Naïve Demand Observations from Inventory Levels

Kaplan–Meier estimation is available in most statistical software packages. In this section, we use the "survival" package in R. Assume that the company's perpetual inventory system tracks inventory level and we remove the restocking policy, but keep the stock-out censoring to impute the demand time-series $q \sim Poisson(\lambda)$ random dataset with $\lambda = 100$ units, right-censor this at $q < 110$ and define demand curve

$D: p = 200 - q + \dfrac{2000}{q}$, which gives us a canonical right concave, downward sloping demand curve. The R-language code that captures this policy would look like this:

```
>quantity = rpois(1000,lambda);>
>hist(quantity);
>price = 200-quantity+(2000/quantity)
>hist(price);

>for(i in 1:1000){
+if(quantity[i] < 110)
+{
+tquantity[i] = quantity[i]
+} else {
+tquantity[i] = 0
+}
+}
```

Under these conditions, the true but unobservable price and quantity frequencies of customer demand follow a Poisson distribution.

Unfortunately, the supply chain manager trying to optimize reorder policy will not see the distributions in price and quantity in Figure 7.4 (because it is unobservable); rather they only have access to look at the "inventory level" derived demand that the supply chain manager would receive (Figure 7.5).

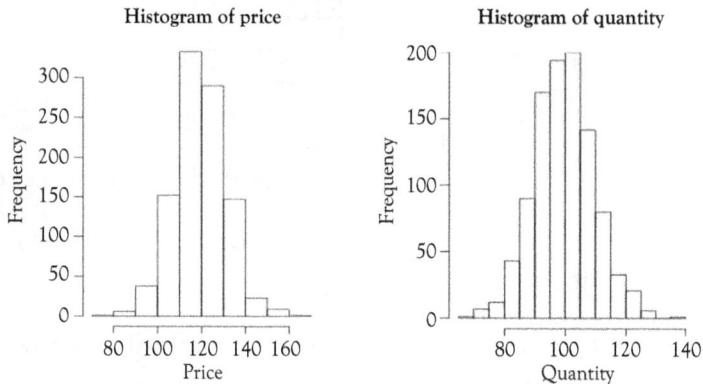

Figure 7.4 Unobservable "true" customer demand price and quantity

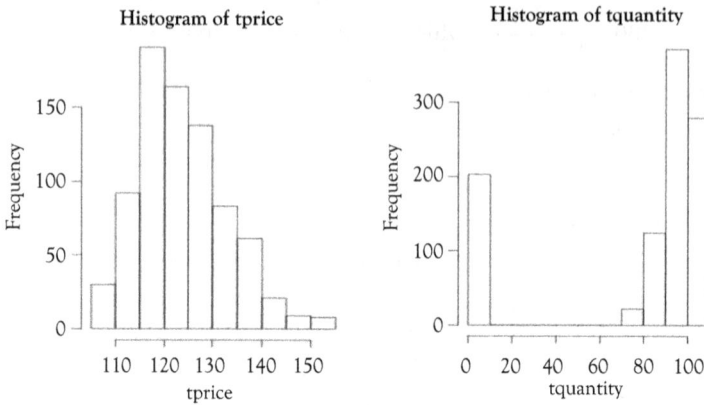

Figure 7.5 Observed customer demand price and quantity

Which can be elicited with the R code:

```
>hist(tquantity);
>tprice = 200-tquantity+(2000/tquantity)
>hist(tprice)
```

None of this is known to the researcher, so we make the order arrival time-series be equivalent to a $t \sim Exponential\left(\frac{1}{\lambda}\right)$ with corresponding truncation; this will create a zero-inflated quantity distribution. The order arrival times V1 and censoring V2 look as follows:

```
>as.data.frame(sdata)
```

	V1	V2
1	6.33E-03	0
2	8.75E-03	1
3	1.00E-03	0
4	1.48E-03	0
...	...	...

And the Kaplan–Meier survival distribution for the quantity is plotted:

```
>fit <- survfit(Surv(sdata[,1],sdata[,2])~1)
>plot(fit)
```

Demand forecasting using inventory level data can itself be extended in a more robust (but potentially less informative) manner using algorithms such as R-language's more precise parametric estimator of the exponential

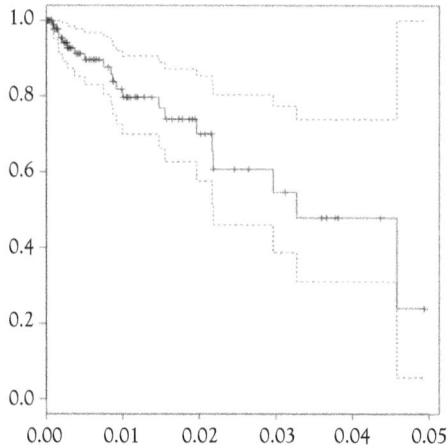

distribution, which can be fitted to data via a BFGS hill-climbing optimization algorithm in the R-language package fitdistrplus. This package allows censored data to contain left-censored, right-censored, and
interval-censored values, with several lower and upper bounds; these
additional capabilities may be desirable in certain real-world situations or
with certain optimization algorithms.

Demand curves in economics are canonically depicted as two-
dimensional price–quantity graphs such as shown in Figure 7.2.
Customer demand, then, will be downward sloping—higher price dis-
courages demand, and results in lower quantity of sales. A supply chain
manager will have access to a price and quantity demand series imputed
from the order (demand) sample observations observed in inventory levels and restocking. We can recover the imputed demand function in a
two-dimensional price–quantity graph using the following R code:

```
>as.data.frame(dmd)
```

	q	P
1	104	115
2	97	124
3	106	113
4	86	137
...	...	...

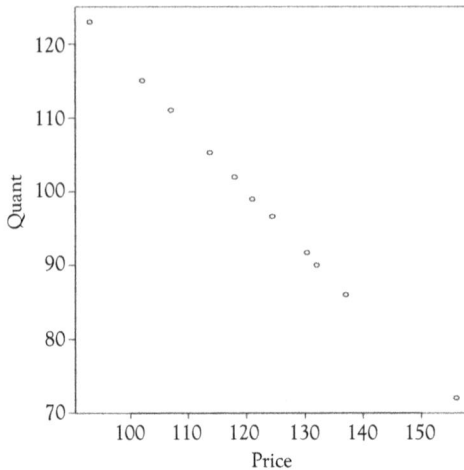

Figure 7.6 Imputed customer demand based on Kaplan–Meier estimation with inventory levels

```
>price=quantile(dmd$p,probs=seq(0,1,.1))
>quant=quantile(dmd$q,probs=seq(1,0,-.1))
>plot(price,quant)
```

The imputed customer demand curve depicted in Figure 7.6 could conceivably provide the basis for a variety of decisions in a corporate environment, and where needed could also recast in a temporal context. Since our approach has isolated inventory levels to provide an optimal estimator of demand, there is little chance of conflating optimization over a specific inventory policy with the estimation of the exogenous "true" customer demand. Such conflation has been a recurrent problem in previous inventory management problems, and implementation of management policy with such conflated algorithms is very likely to generate suboptimal policy implementation. Any conflation of estimation and optimization makes it difficult to discover exactly how much accuracy is sacrificed because of the failure to separate these two problems—a process that wastes scarce customer demand data. The separable Kaplan–Meier estimation should be very robust to a variety of real-world situations, because it is (1) nonparametric, (2) there are a selection of dispersion and fit statistics, and (3) the estimators are efficient, consistent, and unbiased. Copulas can be used to smooth the resulting distributions in accordance to the researcher's assumptions about the real-world demand where small datasets make survival curves too angular and rough.

Using Kaplan–Meier Demand Forecasting Within an Optimization Algorithm

Since the focus of this chapter is only demand forecasting, let's choose a simple and well-known single product inventory management formula familiar to any MBA—the economic order quantity (EOQ). EOQ is the order quantity that minimizes the total holding costs and ordering costs and is one of the oldest classical production scheduling models, initially articulated in Harris [18]. It has a standard solution:

$$q^* = \sqrt{\frac{2\hat{\delta}\kappa}{\eta}}$$

Where $\hat{\delta}$ is the forecasted customer demand for the product; q^* is the optimal reorder quantity for inventory of the product; η represents the inventory carrying cost (e.g., financing, warehouse, refrigeration, insurance, etc.); and κ represents the fixed cost per order and any burn-in, testing, and setup costs associated with receipt of inventory.

Since $\hat{\delta} \pm \epsilon$ will include a forecast error $\pm\epsilon$, the recommended reorder quantity will be a range perhaps associated with some level of confidence or that ours' is a satisfying model, which would have specific implications for risk management and safety stocks. Potential for error $\pm\epsilon$ implies that the real optimum is contained in an interval of width $2\sqrt{\frac{\epsilon\kappa}{\eta}}$:

$$q^* \in \left[\sqrt{\frac{2(\hat{\delta}-\epsilon)\kappa}{\eta}}, \sqrt{\frac{2(\hat{\delta}+\epsilon)\kappa}{\eta}} \right]$$

Harris' EOQ algorithm is relatively simple and can be solved by hand. Moreover, assuming that the demand forecast random variable $\tilde{\delta}$ follows some probability distribution, say a $Normal\left(\hat{\delta}, \sigma_{\hat{\delta}}\right)$ distribution, we can actually compute a distribution for our algorithmic estimator for $q*$. Assume that κ and η are exogenous; then the optimal reorder quantity will be distributed such that $\widetilde{\left(q^*\right)^2} \sim Normal\left(\frac{2\kappa}{\eta}\hat{\delta}, \frac{2\kappa}{\eta}\sigma_{\hat{\delta}}\right)$ and $q*$ will have a χ_1^2-distribution with one degree of freedom. More complex problems will arise, though, when the demand forecast random variable $\widetilde{\widetilde{\delta}}$ needs to be integrated into models with other sources of randomness—for example, in carrying, setup, and other costs. Since the probability of any given demand distribution for separable units of inventory can be defined by a discrete distribution taking only nonnegative integer values with $Pr\ [X = i] = p_i\ (i = 0,1,2\ ...)$, we can use the moment generating function $P(s) = \sum_{i=0}^{\infty} p_i\ s_i$ to uniquely define the distribution. We know that a moment generating function $\sum_{i=0}^{\infty} p_i s_i$ converges uniformly for $|s| \leq 1$. There are many things we can do with moment generating functions that are difficult with random variables, yet they are simpler to use than the more general characteristic functions, which may extend onto the complex plane [20–22]. Differentiating a moment generating function with respect to s, yields the moments of the distribution. Arithmetic functions of random variables have simple generating functions: for example, $\widetilde{X}_1 + \widetilde{X}_2$ has generating function $G_1(s)G_2(s)$. These can significantly simplify the inclusion of demand random variables into complex inventory management optimization algorithms.

References

[1] Forrester, J.W. 1958. "Industrial Dynamics—A Major Breakthrough for Decision Makers." *Harvard Business Review* 36, no. 4, pp. 37–66.

[2] Forrester, J.W. 1976. "Business Structure, Economic Cycles, and National Policy." *Futures* 8, no. 3, pp. 195–214.

[3] Boyle, E., P. Humphreys, and R. McIvor. 2008. "Reducing Supply Chain Environmental Uncertainty Through e-intermediation: An Organization Theory Perspective." *International Journal of Production Economics* 114, no. 1, pp. 347–62.

[4] Moon Mark A., John T. Mentzer, and Dwight E. Thomas. 2000. Customer demand planning at Lucent Technologies – A case study in continuous improvement through sales forecast auditing. Industrial Marketing Management 29, pp. 19–26.

[5] Reyes, P.M., G.V. Frazier, E.L. Prater, and A.R. Cannon. 2007. "RFID: The State of the Union Between Promise and Practice." *International Journal of Integrated Supply Management* 3, no. 2, pp. 192–206.

[6] Reyes, P.M., and G.V. Frazier. 2007. "Radio Frequency Identification: Past, Present and Future Business Applications." *International Journal of Integrated Supply Management* 3, no. 2, pp. 125–34.

[7] Zhao, X., J. Xie, and R.S.M. Lau. 2001. "Improving the Supply Chain Performance: Use of Forecasting Models versus Early Order Commitments." *International Journal of Production Research* 39, no. 17, pp. 3923–39.

[8] Zhao, X., J. Xie, and J. Leung. 2002. "The Impact of Forecasting Model Selection on the Value of Information Sharing in a Supply Chain." *European Journal of Operational Research* 142, no. 2, pp. 321–44.

[9] Bayraktar, E., S.C. Lenny Koh, A. Gunasekaran, K. Sari, and E. Tatoglu. 2008. "The Role of Forecasting on Bullwhip Effect for E-SCM Applications." *International Journal of Production Economics* 113, no. 1, pp. 193–204.

[10] Wright, D., and X. Yuan. 2008. "Mitigating the Bullwhip Effect by Ordering Policies and Forecasting Methods." *International Journal of Production Economics* 113, no. 2, pp. 587–97.

[11] Albertson, K., and J. Aylen. 2003. "Forecasting the Behavior of Manufacturing Inventory." *International Journal of Forecasting* 19, no. 2, pp. 299–311.

[12] Chatfield, C., and M. Yar. 1988. "Holt-Winters Forecasting: Some Practical Issues." *The Statistician* 37, no. 2, pp. 129–40.

[13] Huh, W.T., R. Levi, P. Rusmevichientong, and J.B. Orlin. 2011. "Adaptive Data-Driven Inventory Control with Censored Demand Based on Kaplan–Meier Estimator." *Operations Research* 59, no. 4, pp. 929–41.

[14] Edgeworth, F.Y. 1888. "The Mathematical Theory of Banking." *Journal of the Royal Statistical Society* 51, no. 1, pp. 113–27. JSTOR 2979084.

[15] Arrow, K.J., T. Harris, and J. Marshak. 1951. "Optimal Inventory Policy." *Econometrica* 19, no. 3, pp. 250–72.

[16] Samartzis, L. 2006. Survival and Censored Data (No. STAT-REPORT-2007-001).

[17] Gill, R. 1983. "Large Sample Behaviour of the Product-Limit Estimator on the Whole Line." *The Annals of Statistics* 11, no. 1, pp. 49–58.

[18] Harris, F.W. 1915. "Operations and Cost." Factory Management Series, pp. 48–52. Chicago: Shaw.

[19] Fleming, T.H., and D.P. Harrington. 1984. "Nonparametric Estimation of the Survival Distribution in Censored Data." Comm. in Statistics 13, no. 20, pp. 2469–86.

[20] Towill, D.R. 2005. "The Impact of Business Policy on Bullwhip Induced Risk in Supply Chain Management." *International Journal of Physical Distribution and Logistics Management* 35, no. 8, pp. 555–75.

[21] Hines, P., M. Holweg, and J. Sullivan. 2000. "Waves, Beaches, Breakwaters and Rip Currents—A Three-Dimensional View of Supply Chain Dynamics." *International Journal of Physical Distribution and Logistics Management* 30, no. 10, pp. 827–46.

[22] Holweg, M., and J. Bicheno. 2016. "The Reverse Amplification Effect in Supply Chains." *Developments in Logistics and Supply Chain Management*, eds. K.S. Pawar, H. Rogers, A. Potter, and M. Naim, 52–58. Berlin, Germany: Springer.

[23] Kaplan, E.L., P. Meier. 1958. "Nonparametric Estimation from Incomplete Observations." *Journal of the American Statistical Association* 53, no. 282, pp. 457–81. JSTOR 2281868.

CHAPTER 8

Public–Private Partnerships (PPP) in Transportation: An Analysis of Alternatives

Anthony M. Pagano[*]

Public–private partnerships (PPPs) are in the forefront of approaches to funding transportation infrastructure improvements. Highlighted in the highway area by long-term leases of the Chicago Skyway and Indiana Toll Road, a variety of states are investigating the use of PPPs either as "Brownfield" leases like the Chicago and Indiana cases, or "Greenfield" Design, Build, Operate, Transfer arrangements. These and other PPP projects raise a variety of issues, including the length of the lease, toll escalation permitted, and use of funds. This chapter develops a rationale for PPPs in transportation, evaluates several approaches to PPPs using this rationale, and analyzes some of the difficult issues that can surface.

Introduction

The world of public–private partnerships (PPPs) changed in the United States in 2004 with the Chicago Skyway long-term lease agreement. In exchange for an upfront payment of $1.83 billion, the Skyway Concession Company comprised of Cintra and Macquarie Infrastructure Group will operate the facility for 99 years. This lease was followed in 2005 with

* Reprinted from the *Journal of the Transportation Research Forum*, Volume 49, Number 2, Summer 2010. Reprinted with permission from the Transportation Research Forum.

the lease of the Indiana Toll Road. The deal involved an upfront payment of $3.8 billion to the State of Indiana for the right to operate the road for 75 years [1]. The city of Chicago has been pursuing a lease of Midway Airport. These types of deals are numerous in Europe and developing countries, but have not been used very much in the United States. This chapter develops a rationale for PPPs in transportation, evaluates several approaches to PPPs using this rationale, and analyzes some of the difficult issues that surface.

The Rationale for Public Involvement in Transportation Decisions

In order to understand the rationale for PPPs in transportation, it is necessary to begin with an understanding of the rationale for public involvement in transportation decisions. To begin, it is necessary to make a distinction between government involvement in transportation decisions and public provision of transportation facilities and services. Government involvement does not mean that government must actively develop and operate transportation facilities. A variety of reasons can be cited for government involvement in transportation decisions. These reasons center on market failure in transportation markets. This means if left to the private sector only, transportation services would not be produced in socially optimal amounts.

One reason for government involvement concerns the nature of transportation markets. Either because of institutional reasons, the lumpiness of productive factors used to produce transportation, or because of decreasing costs with greater density along given routes, free entry into the production of transportation facilities and services may be precluded to the point that monopoly may result. Without governmental involvement, market forces may fail to provide an optimal allocation of resources to transportation. Exclusive private provision may result in only one or a few providers, producing a level and quality of transportation services that is less than desirable.

A second reason concerns the externalities resulting from transportation, both positive and negative. These include land-use impacts, economic development impacts, and air, noise, and water pollution, among others. If left solely to private providers, the social costs and benefits of transportation may not be fully taken into account. To the extent that transportation services are public goods, then public involvement in transportation decisions can be justified as a third reason. Public goods have two characteristics that result in lack of private supply in adequate amounts. The first characteristic is nonexclusion. Individuals can be excluded from the consumption of private goods provided by the free market if they do not pay for them. The characteristic of nonexclusion means that if private business would attempt to supply public goods, they could not obtain payment from all consumers of the service. Although altruism may motivate some businesses, the lack of adequate revenues is a powerful deterrent to private provision of transportation services.

The second characteristic of public goods is joint supply. This means that if the good or service is provided to one individual, it is jointly provided to everyone. The marginal cost of supplying one additional consumer is very low or zero. If price is set equal to marginal cost, private provision would not be forthcoming.

Other reasons for government involvement include the high risk and payback periods associated with large transportation projects, equity considerations (providing access to employment opportunities, shopping, and other opportunities), and the mobility options provided by access to alternative modes of transportation.

These reasons suggest that government should be involved in decisions concerning transportation facility and service levels. The public sector may need to subsidize some services. It should also participate in the planning and coordination of such services.

Rationale for Public Production of Transportation Services

While a case for government involvement in transportation decisions can be made, it is less obvious why government should be involved in the actual production of transportation services.

First, some functions require such elaborate supervision that even if they were produced by private firms, the situation would be the equivalent of public production. In his classic book on public finance, Musgrave [2] cites the operations of military establishments and the administration of justice as examples. Services such as these require close control on the part of the electorate or representatives of the people in a democratic society. However, transportation is not quite like the military, police, or the courts. The necessity for close supervision does not seem to be a valid reason to justify public operation of transportation facilities.

A second reason for public production of transportation services concerns the problems of natural monopoly. Public production is an alternative to regulated or unregulated private monopoly. This justification rests on the premise that public production results in better outcomes than the other two alternatives. It is a matter of judgment whether this premise is correct.

Inertia may also explain why some services are produced in the public sector. Education and the postal monopoly are good examples.

As can be seen from this discussion, public production of services in general, and production of transportation services in particular, may not be justified in many situations.

Rationale for Private Sector Involvement

An important question to ask is why would private sector involvement be more desirable? The answer centers on the two types of efficiency. Allocative efficiency exists if resources are devoted to the highest value in use. In the case of transportation, allocative efficiency exists if the amount and quality of transportation produced is at an optimal level. Allocative efficiency thus concerns what and how much to produce. The previous discussion of why government should be involved in transportation decisions involves allocative efficiency.

The second type of efficiency is called productive, managerial, cost, or X-efficiency in Leibenstein's [3] terms. Efficiency in this sense implies that production is maximized for a given level of inputs.

This type of efficiency is concerned not with how much to produce, but rather with how to produce it. A given level of transportation is provided efficiently in this sense if production costs are minimized.

In the private sector, competitive forces and the desire to maximize profit and stay in business provide incentives for firms to achieve this second type of efficiency. In a purely competitive situation, only those firms that have maximized cost efficiency can survive.

In the public sector, on the other hand, the incentives to achieve efficiency in the provision of public services are indirect. Incentives are provided through the political system by voters, legislators, and appointed commissions. If efficiency in the provision of these services is not achieved, then this indirect process may take some time to make adjustments. In many situations, adequate adjustments may never be made.

This indirect process may involve voting a party or elected official out of office. However, many issues are usually involved in a decision as to which candidate to vote for. Waste and inefficiency in the provision of public services may be hidden under an array of other problems and issues. The process may also involve legislatures passing laws that attempt to provide incentives for the efficient administration of government programs. However, dedicated public administrators must implement these laws and deal with an entrenched bureaucracy protected by civil service status. This bureaucracy may remain largely unaffected by attempts to streamline public programs.

Special commissions perform studies and make recommendations to produce government services more efficiently. However, in many cases, these reports seem to end up on a bookshelf rather than being implemented. The problem is that the direct incentives of profit, loss, and competition in the private sector are not present in the public sector.

Rationale for Public–Private Partnerships

This discussion suggests that a combination of public–private sector involvement in transportation would result in a better achievement of both types of efficiencies. If sole reliance is placed on the private sector, market failure may result. Allocative efficiency may not be attained. If sole reliance is placed on government to provide transportation services, cost efficiency may not result.

However, if the public sector maintains a role in transportation such as planning, coordination, and possibly subsidy, and the private sector is used to actually operate the system, then possibly both types of efficiency could be attained. This is especially true if private sector partners can be obtained through competitive markets or a competitive bid process.

This PPP is what Osborne and Gaebler [4] called Steering vs. Rowing. In their view, government and the private sector should specialize in what each sector does best. Government is best at steering—deciding what to produce, how much to produce, and allocating resources to production. The private sector is best in actually producing the service. Each sector specializes in its core business function.

There are other rationales for PPPs that include capital shortages of financially strapped jurisdictions, ability to access value in the facility, the ability to raise tolls independent of political considerations, and transfer of risk from the public sector to the private. For details on the kinds of risks that can be transferred, see FHWA [5]. The implementation of a PPP based on these rationales may also have an effect on both allocative and cost efficiency potential.

Types of Public–Private Partnerships

There are a variety of PPPs that have been practiced in transportation. Some are designed to achieve the allocative and X-efficiency goals outlined earlier. Others, however, may have far different motivations. Table 8.1 shows a categorization of alternative PPP approaches to the provision of transportation services. This table shows broad categories of approaches. Within each category, there could be several alternative ways in which the public and private sectors interact.

The first approach is Design Build. The private sector designs and constructs the new facility. The public sector role is planning, operation, and subsidy of the facility. This is the classic approach to PPPs by which most of the highway system in the United States was constructed. The second approach is Build, Operate Transfer (BOT) or Design, Build, Operate Transfer (DBOT).

In this approach, the private sector builds, operates, finances, and maintains the facility, and then over a period of years, transfers the facility to the public sector. This is called a "Greenfield Concession" since a brand new facility is built. There are a variety of roles that the private sector can play in this type of PPP. The private sector can finance the facility or financing can be done by the public sector. One important question is should these roles be performed by the same or different firms. Marimort and Pouyet [6] analyze whether building infrastructure and managing

Table 8.1 Alternative public–private partnership approaches in transportation

Approach	Private sector role	Public sector role
1. Design Build	Design and Construction of Facility	Planning, Operation, and Subsidy of Facility
2. Build, Operate Transfer (BOT) or DBOT—Greenfield Concession	Build, Operate, Finance, Maintain, Transfer	Negotiation with private companies, regulation, contract enforcement, quality assurance
3. Long-term Lease of Existing Facility—Brownfield Concession	Finance, Operate, Maintain, Transfer	Negotiation with private companies, regulation, contract enforcement, quality assurance
4. Competitive Contracting	Operation and Maintenance	Negotiation with private companies, regulation, contract enforcement, quality assurance, subsidy
5. Asset Sales	Finance, Operate, Maintain	Negotiation with private companies or no role
6. Vouchers	Finance, Operate, Maintain	Negotiation with private companies, subsidy, quality assurance
7. Deregulation	Build, Operate, Finance, Maintain	None
8. Publicization	Build, Operate, Finance, Maintain	Planning, Subsidy

assets should be bundled or not. They conclude that a technology-driven reason is the basis for this decision.

The public sector is involved in negotiation with private companies, possible regulation of prices, contract enforcement, and quality assurance. This approach has been widely used in developing countries where there is a capital scarcity. The length of the concession can vary up to 99 years. Most typical are concessions that last for 30–50 years. Details on various alternatives within this approach can be found in Buxbaum and Ortiz [7].

A long-term lease of an existing facility, called a "Brownfield Concession," is the third approach. This is the approach that has gained much notoriety after the leases of the Chicago Skyway and the Indiana Toll Road. The possible lease of Midway Airport is also this type. The Chicago

Skyway lease was the first in the United States. This type of PPP has raised many questions, which will be discussed later in this chapter.

Competitive Contracting is the fourth approach. In this approach, the public sector contracts with the private sector to operate and maintain a service. The public sector is involved in negotiation with the private sector, regulation, contract enforcement, quality assurance, and subsidy of the service. This type of PPP is prevalent in public transit throughout the country, including service in Denver, Phoenix, Los Angeles suburbs, and Chicago suburbs. Much of the paratransit service in the United States is provided through this approach. For a discussion of a variety of contracted services in transit, see Richmond [8].

The fifth approach is Asset Sales. This approach is used to privatize state-owned enterprises (SOEs). The private sector takes the role of financing, operating, and maintaining the facility. The public sector role is either to negotiate a sales price with private companies or no role. There are two types of asset sales. One is a Citizen Share Purchase, in which the asset is sold to an individual company or shares are sold in the marketplace. In this approach, the government keeps all the proceeds from the sale. The privatization of Conrail was done in this manner. The second approach is called "Voucher Privatization" by Pool [9]. In this approach, the SOE is privatized by distributing shares to citizens of the country. Citizens are free to sell or keep their shares. In this case, the proceeds from the sale accrue to individuals rather than to the government. British Columbia used this approach in the privatization of its state-owned forest products and natural gas companies. Pool [9] notes that this approach was also used by the Czech Republic in privatizing its SOEs. Asset sales are similar to "Brownfield Concessions," except that the facility is permanently transferred to the private sector.

The next PPP approach is Vouchers. In this approach, vouchers are provided to users of the service to purchase the service from private operators. Private companies are responsible for all aspects of their service, while the public sector negotiates with the private companies on the basis of price and quality of service. The public sector also subsidizes the service and monitors quality. This approach has been used extensively in paratransit operations in the United States and in school vouchers in several cities.

In Deregulation, the public sector allows private competition with a formerly monopoly public sector operation. The private sector is responsible for all aspects of their service, while the public sector plays no role in the private sector operation. The U.S. postal service, which allows competition from FedEx and UPS for overnight and package delivery, is a good example of this approach. While not necessarily a PPP, the private sector competition can result in the public sector becoming more efficient and effective in the provision of its services.

The last PPP approach can be called "Publicization." In this approach, the public sector becomes involved in what was an exclusive private operation. Publicization is not nationalization, since there is a very large role played by the private sector. Examples include the CREATE project in Chicago, where the public sector is working with the railroads to reduce time spent in the Chicago terminal, and the Wisconsin and Southern Railroad in Wisconsin, in which the state has acquired the trackage on which the private railroad operates. Other examples include the Alemeda Corridor project in Southern California, the BNSF Flyover in Kansas, the FAST project in the state of Washington, and the Sauk Village Logisticenter development in suburban Chicago. In each of these cases, the public sector has become involved in what has traditionally been a strictly private sector endeavor to build, maintain, and operate freight transportation infrastructure. Also included in this category are various approaches to transit-oriented development and joint development agreements.

Other PPP approaches are strictly financial, such as Business Improvement Districts (BID), which involves assessing businesses that are adjacent to a transportation development, and Tax Increment Financing (TIF), in which increased property tax revenues pay for current infrastructure investment [5].

Evaluation of the Alternative Approaches

Given the variety of alternative PPPs, the next question is how well do each of these achieve society's transportation goals. In order to answer this question, each approach is analyzed for its potential in achieving allocative and cost efficiency. This potential may or may not be achieved in practice. However, it is more likely that efficient operations would result

Table 8.2 Evaluation of public–private partnership approaches in transportation

Approach	Allocative efficiency potential	Cost efficiency potential
1. Design Build	Excellent	Poor
2. Build, Operate Transfer (BOT) or DBOT— Greenfield Concession	Depends on Specifics of the Contract	Excellent
3. Long-term Lease of Existing Facility— Brownfield Concession	Depends on Specifics of the Contract	Excellent
4. Competitive Contracting	Excellent	Excellent
5. Asset Sales	Good—Depends on Details	Good
6. Vouchers	Excellent	Excellent
7. Deregulation	Excellent	Good to Poor
8. Publicization	Excellent	Good

if a high potential approach were implemented, rather than one with poor potential. The results of this analysis are shown in Table 8.2.

The potential for an approach to achieve allocative efficiency would be present if the alternative has a strong potential to achieve an optimal allocation of resources to transportation services. This includes the potential to take externalities into account in production decisions, the public goods nature of some facilities, and the avoidance of private monopoly. In addition, allocative efficiency results if equity considerations can be dealt with and if the approach can provide a funding mechanism for large, risky projects with long payback periods. Cost efficiency potential is present if the implementation of an approach results in the creation of incentives to be efficient.

Each of the approaches is ranked as excellent, good, or poor in potential to achieve these efficiencies. For allocative efficiency, excellent implies that implementing an approach will most likely lead to effective use of resources in transportation. The socially desirable amount and type of transportation has the best chance of being achieved under these alternatives. Allocative efficiency is ranked as good if the alternative can lead to a social optimum in transportation, but this really depends on the details of the contract between the public and private sectors.

A cost efficiency potential is ranked according to the extent to which incentives to be efficient are present in an alternative. Excellent implies that market mechanisms are operating efficiently in that alternative. Alternatives ranked as good imply that the market may have an effect on cost efficiency, but other factors such as monopoly provision may hinder cost efficiency goals. Those ranked as poor imply that political rather than market mechanisms determine the efficiency of delivery of services.

The traditional approach, Design Build, involves the public sector actually planning, operating, and subsidizing the facility. The private sector role is design and construction of the facility. The allocative efficiency potential is excellent since the public sector can deal with externalities, public goods effects, and equity. However, the cost efficiency potential is quite low. The incentives to be efficient are indirect with this approach.

Greenfield Concessions have been used for many years in less developed countries. They directly deal with the problem of capital scarcity by being able to access private capital markets. The cost efficiency potential is excellent, since the incentives of the marketplace are at work in this approach. However, the allocative efficiency potential depends on the specifics of the contract with the private sector. This is also the case for the Brownfield Concession approach. However, both these approaches raise many troubling issues that must be dealt with. In the next section of this chapter, several of these issues will be discussed.

Approach 4 is Competitive Contracting. This approach has an excellent potential to achieve both types of efficiencies. The public sector can take a large role in planning services, internalizing external effects, and taking equity considerations and other allocative efficiency effects into account. Relying on competitive bids, inefficient operators would be underbid by better-managed firms. As long as many operators are competing, the potential for cost efficiency is excellent.

Asset sales have a good chance of achieving both allocative efficiency and cost efficiency goals. However, like Greenfield and Brownfield Concessions, the devil is in the details. If the sale results in monopoly private operation of the facility, then cost efficiency goals may not be fully obtained. However, if the SOE is highly inefficient, with many layers of bureaucracy and unneeded workers and infused with corruption, then a private monopoly may be preferable. Allocative efficiency potential depends on a variety of details, including the amount and type of government regulation.

Since Vouchers rely on the public sector to do the "Steering" and the private sector to do the "Rowing" the potential for achieving both allocative and cost efficiency goals are excellent.

Deregulation, approach 7, can lead to excellent allocative efficiency potential since both the private sector and the public sector are providing the service. However, since the public sector is providing a competing service, cost efficiency can suffer because of the lack of incentives for the public sector operation to be efficient, especially if the public operation is subsidized.

Finally, Publicization has the potential to achieve allocative efficiencies since the public sector involvement can take a variety of external effects into account, including economic development and pollution. Cost efficiency potential is good since the private sector is still very actively involved in the provision of service.

Some Difficult Issues

There are many difficult issues that must be dealt with in the implementation of PPPs. In this section of the chapter, a few of these issues will be discussed. This is not a comprehensive list. The focus is on problems that affect Greenfield and Brownfield concessions.

Length of the Contract Period

The first issue concerns the length of the contract period. This is especially the case for Brownfield Concessions. The Chicago Skyway concession is for 99 years. The Indiana Toll Road contract period is 75 years. The Midway Airport concession was proposed to last for 99 years. Private companies prefer a longer payback period for two reasons. One is that the company has a longer period in which to earn revenues to offset the initial investment. Second, for tax purposes, the Internal Revenue Service (IRS) treats such a long-term lease as ownership of the facility. The company can then depreciate investments as if they own the facility. So, private sector risk is reduced, the longer the length of the contract.

From a public sector standpoint, the longer the contract period, the more likely the facility will be able to generate higher upfront payments. But there is a risk involved for longer contract periods. There are many societal, technological, and developmental changes that can occur in 99 years. Suppose a facility was leased in 1910, with a 99-year lease, coming due in 2009. The United States is fundamentally different in almost all aspects over those 99 years. A facility that was leased in 1910 could stand in the way of new development today. So could be the result in 2108, when a 99-year lease written today would be completed. The public sector may have new uses for the facility that may not be easily implemented if it is in private hands. This risk can be mitigated through the use of contract language that gives the public sector the right to purchase the lease at fair market value in the future. This, however, may lower the amount that firms would be willing to pay upfront. Additionally, in the long term, technology or development patterns may make the facility obsolete. This could affect the private sector risk in the later years of the lease as well.

The private firm that is leasing the facility would prefer a longer contract period to a shorter one. However, the present value of earnings far in the future will be less than near-term earnings. Thus, the private profitability curve flattens out over very long contract periods. The present value of the future income stream can be greater, the greater the amount of cost efficiency savings from private ownership.

To the extent that the public sector can bargain away some of these savings, the initial lease payment will be larger and the time that it takes to recoup the lease payment will be longer.

To simplify the analysis, let us assume an initial lease payment with constant revenues and operations costs each year. Then let:

L = the lease payment

R = yearly revenues from the lease

C_f = yearly costs of operating the facility for the firm

n = length of the contract period

r = appropriate private sector discount factor

t = time

TP_n = Present value of profit stream to be derived from operating the lease over n years

Then:

$$TP_n = \sum_{t=1}^{n} \frac{R - C_{f-L}}{(1+r)^t} \qquad (8.1)$$

The total profit that accrues to the private company leasing the facility is a transfer from road users to the company. It can be considered the total social cost of the lease. This is not the social cost of operating the facility. Rather, it is the social cost of leasing the facility to a private company. This is shown in Figure 8.1 as TP_n. As shown in the figure, the present value of the total profits to be derived from leasing the facility increases at a decreasing rate, reflecting the declining present value of profits over time. Point B in the figure is the breakeven number of years of the lease.

A reasonable approximation to the marginal profits accruing to the firm of leasing the facility for one more year is:

$$MP_t = \frac{R - C_f}{(1+r)^t} \qquad (8.2)$$

This is shown in the figure as MP_t. Marginal profits, and thus the marginal social cost of leasing the facility, decline over time. In making decisions as to the total upfront lease payment, and the length of the contract period, the private sector firm would use this function in the process of negotiation.

The marginal social cost of a private firm operating the facility for one more year is equal to the marginal profits plus the yearly cost of operation.

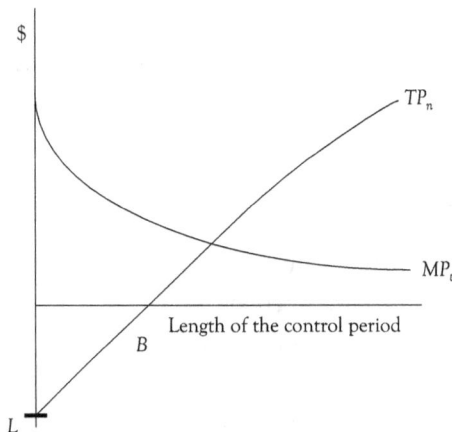

Figure 8.1 Present value of future private sector profits from lease

So:

$$MSC_t = \frac{R}{(1+r)^t} \qquad (8.3)$$

Society benefits from the operation of the facility. Initially, the public sector receives the lease payment L from the private company. This payment could include any cost efficiency gains that are bargained away from the private contractor. In addition, there is the continuation of an allocative efficiency gain from continual use of the facility. However, this allocative efficiency gain declines over time. The allocative efficiency gains are discounted by the appropriate social rate of discount and by a risk factor as alternative uses for the facility develop. Thus, the total public sector benefit curve declines over time as the length of the contract is extended. To simplify, assume that the allocative efficiency gains are a constant amount over time, and that the social discount factor is the same as the private sector discount factor. Then:

$$SB_n = \sum_{t=1}^{n} \frac{AE}{(1+r+U)^t} + L \qquad (8.4)$$

where:

SB_n = Total Social Benefits from leasing the facility

AE = Allocative Efficiency gains from the use of the facility

U = Public sector risk factor

Then the marginal social benefits of leasing the facility are given by:

$$MSB_t = \frac{AE}{(1+r+U)^t} \qquad (8.5)$$

Marginal social benefits and costs are shown in Figure 8.2. Initially, allocative efficiency benefits from the use of the facility are greater than the private sector costs of operation of the facility. Otherwise, the facility would be abandoned. Both benefits and costs of operation decline, the longer the facility is operated. This is shown as the declining curves in the figure. However, as displayed in the figure, MSB_t declines at a faster rate than MSC_t, reflecting the public sector risk factor. If the public sector risk factor is very low, the two functions may not intersect for many if

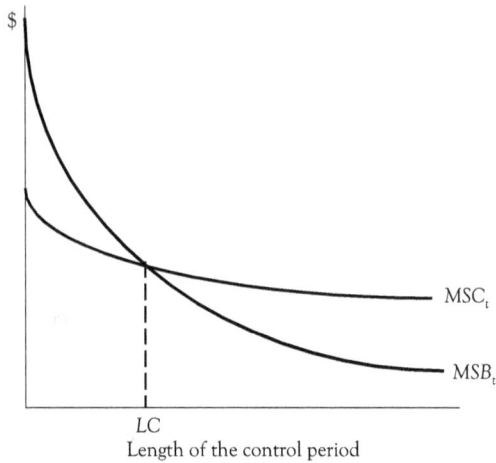

Figure 8.2 Socially optimal contract period

not hundreds of years. In that case, the facility is best sold to the private sector as an asset sale.

The optimal length of the contract is shown as the intersection of these two lines, *LC*. If the length of the contract is less than this, it would be advantageous to expand the contract length. Contract periods greater than *LC* would involve a social loss. Depending on the public sector risk factor, contract periods of 75–99 years may not be socially desirable. For example, PIROG has argued that contracts should be no longer than 30 years [10]. While this may be too short for some concessions to break even, it indicates that the longer contract periods may not be beneficial. Ortiz and Buxbaum [1] note that in other countries, concession agreements are typically for 30–40 years.

The Chicago Skyway concession agreement allows for toll increases after the first five years. The increases can be at the highest of 2 percent per annum, increase in the consumer price index (CPI) or increase in nominal gross domestic product (GDP) [11]. Each of these possible toll increases results in a different revenue stream for the private contractor and thus a different marginal social cost function. This is shown in Figure 8.3. In the figure, it is assumed that nominal GDP growth is greater than the CPI, which is greater than 2 percent. The greater the toll increases allowed, the greater the total revenues generated and the shorter the optimal contract period. If traffic grows at faster rates, thus generating more revenues, then the optimal length

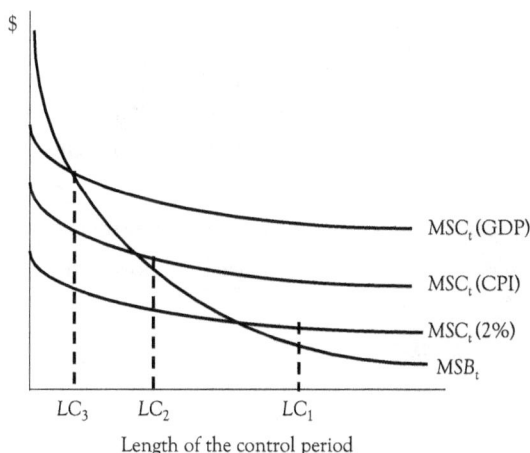

Figure 8.3 Toll increases and optimal length of the contract period

of the contract would be less. However, increases in traffic may also result in increased operating costs, thus changing the cost function.

This analysis assumes that public sector decision makers attempt to maximize social welfare. This may not always be the case. Maskin and Tirole [12] consider situations when government officials have preferences that differ from those of a social welfare maximizer, such as preference for pork barrel projects. They develop a model to analyze the implications of these situations and suggest ways in which the negative effects on social welfare can be minimized.

Use of Funds from Initial Lease Payment

If a Greenfield Concession is implemented, the initial costs of the project are utilized to design and build the planned facility. Brownfield Concessions are different. A large upfront lease payment is made to the government entity by the private company. The government entity could use the proceeds for other transportation improvements or to pay for general government. There is a tendency to view this large payment as a windfall to be used to balance budgets, pay down debt, or fund new government services. In the case of the Chicago Skyway, proceeds were used to repay project debt, create reserve accounts, and provide for programs unrelated to transportation. The Indiana Toll Road proceeds were completely dedicated to funding a 10-year transportation capital program [13].

The lease payment must be paid back to the private company over time by users of the facility. If it is used to finance transportation improvements, then users of the facility help to finance improvements elsewhere in the system. On the other hand, if the proceeds are used for general government, then users of the facility in the future will pay for general government today. This is an intergenerational transfer that may not be socially desirable, especially since users of the facility years hence have no say in the matter.

Noncompete Provisions

Several of the contracts have noncompete provisions, giving the private sector contractor a monopoly over the provision of the service. The inclusion of these provisions is a two-edged sword. On the one hand, some of the market power that is transferred to private hands can be bargained away and may result in larger upfront payments, especially for Brownfield Concessions. On the other hand, such market power can lead to much higher tolls over time. Thus, it may be necessary to counter such provisions with strict price regulation, which carries a whole host of problems that are well documented in the public utility literature.

In the case of the Chicago Skyway, alternative routes currently exist, but are very circuitous. The existence of these routes would tend to keep a cap on toll increases. There are several alternatives to Midway Airport, including O'Hare, Mitchell Airport in Milwaukee, and Gary Airport, which currently has no commercial service, but could host such service in the future. The Peotone Airport, which has been a source of contention for many years, could also serve as an alternative. Thus, there exists much potential competition for a Midway Airport concession outside the city of Chicago. There are slower, but more scenic alternatives to the Indiana Toll Road, so competition already exists. Thus, in these three cases, noncompete provisions would have little or no practical effect.

Facilities Requiring Subsidy

Public transit offers unique problems with regard to PPPs. These facilities usually require subsidy, so it would not seem feasible to ask private operators to engage in a long-term concession and pay an upfront fee. After all, who would pay to operate a money-losing facility? The usual approaches in public transit are competitive contracting or vouchers, in which the private operator receives compensation from the public transit provider to operate routes or facilities.

One approach that has been used in the United Kingdom is an "Availability Payment." The private company is responsible for one or more functions of design, build, finance, operate, and maintain a "Greenfield" project. In return, the public agency provides a monthly payment to the company during the operations and maintenance phase of the project. In the United States, this approach has been used in the Port of Miami truck tunnel project. The FTA has selected three cities (Denver, Houston, and Bay Area) to implement such PPP projects [14].

There are possibilities for other forms of PPPs in public transit as well. One alternative is for the private company to pay an upfront fee to the public transit provider to operate an existing route or facility for a certain number of years. The private operator could control the fares charged with government vouchers for low-income riders, receive an agreed-upon shadow fare for each customer served, or receive an availability payment. A shadow fare is a payment to the private operator usually on a per-rider basis as compensation for providing the service. Typically, it would exceed the actual fare collected. Shadow fares provide an incentive to increase ridership.

Such approaches have not been tried in the United States, but may offer many of the benefits of PPPs to transit.

Conclusions

PPPs offer the prospect of achieving desired social benefits of transportation in the most efficient manner possible. The planning, coordination, and possibly subsidy provided by the public sector are combined with the incentives of the free market. There are a variety of approaches to PPPs, which have been implemented either in the United States or in other countries. Most offer outstanding prospects of achieving both allocative and cost efficiency goals. The most problematic approach is the "Brownfield Concession," which is most well-known today. However, with carefully crafted agreements, shorter contract periods, and upfront payments that are used to enhance transportation, such an approach can also achieve social goals at lowest cost.

References

[1] Ortiz, I.N., and J.N. Buxbaum. 2008. "Protecting the Public Interest in Long-Term Concession Agreements for Transportation Infrastructure." *Public Works Management and Policy* 13, no. 2, pp. 126–137.

[2] Musgrave, R.A. 1959. *The Theory of Public Finance*. New York, NY: McGraw Hill.

[3] Leibenstein, H. 1966. "Allocative Efficiency vs. 'X-Efficiency." *American Economic Review* 56, no. 3, pp. 392–415.

[4] Osborne, D., and T. Gaebler. 1993. *Reinventing Government: How the Entrepreneurial Spirit Is Transforming the Public Sector*. New York, NY: Penguin Books.

[5] FHWA. 2007. User Guidebook on Implementing Public–Private Partnerships for Transportation Infrastructure Projects in the United States. Final Report, July 2007. www.fhwa.dot.gov/ipd/p3/

[6] Martimort, D., and J. Pouyet. 2008. "To Build or Not to Build: Normative and Positive Theories of Public–Private Partnerships." *International Journal of Industrial Organization* 26, no. 2, pp. 393–411.

[7] Buxbaum, J., and I. Ortiz. 2009. "Public-Sector Decision Making for Public–Private Partnerships: A Synthesis of Highway Practice." *NCHRP Synthesis* 391. Washington, D.C: Transportation Research Board.

[8] Richmond, J. 2001. "*The Private Provision of Public Transport*. Cambridge, MA: Harvard University Taubman Center for State and Local Government.

[9] Pool, R.W. Jr. 1996. "Privatization for Economic Development." In *The Privatization Process: A Worldwide Perspective*, eds. T.L. Anderson and P.J. Hill, 1–18. London: Rowman and Littefield Publishers.

[10] Baxandall, P. 2007. *Road Privatization: Explaining the Trend, Assessing the Facts, and Protecting the Public*. Boston, MA: U.S. PIRG Education Fund.

[11] Enright, D. 2006. *The Chicago Skyway Sale: An Analytical Review*. Chicago, IL: NW Financial Group, LLC.

[12] Maskin, E., and J. Tirole. 2008. "Public–Private Partnerships and Government Spending Limits." *International Journal of Industrial Organization* 26, no. 2, pp. 412–20.

[13] FHWA. 2009. *Public Policy Considerations in Public–Private Partnership (PPP) Arrangements*. www.fhwa.dot.gov.

[14] Fishman, E. 2009. "Will Private Investment in Public Transit Fill the Funding Gap?" *Metro Magazine,* January 8. www.metro-magazine.com/Magazine/Current-Issue.aspx

About the Authors

Matthew Liotine is a professor in Information Decision Sciences at the University of Illinois at Chicago (UIC). He is a renowned expert in the field of operations management and supply chain planning, and is an industry consultant. At UIC, he teaches courses in operations and supply chain management, enterprise resource planning, quality control and information systems. His prime research interest is in the area of supply chain data science. He is the recipient of the UIC Teaching Recognition Award and is a Teaching Learning Scholar. He is also a founder and director of UIC's Certificate Program in Emergency Management and Continuity Planning.

Dr. Liotine was formally the Chair of the Academic Program Committee for the Information Systems Audit and Control Association (ISACA) and is a former president of INFORMS for the Chicago region. He served in several professional positions, including technical manager at AT&T Bell Laboratories, where he pioneered intelligent networks and flexible network routing methods, originated the concept of full group engineering, and was the recipient of the AT&T Network Architecture Award and AT&T Quality Award. In other roles, he was a senior staff engineer at Union Carbide's Linde Division, where he founded that company's National Logistics Center. He also developed and managed a systems integration practice for the Carlson Group, and was an Associate Vice President at Edwards & Kelcey, Inc.

He has over 40 publications and is the author of the bestseller "Mission Critical Network Planning." He holds PhD, MA, and MS degrees in engineering and operations research from Princeton University, and MS and BS degrees in engineering from New York University's Polytechnic Institute.

Anthony M. Pagano, PhD is Director of the Center for Supply Chain Management and Logistics (www.supply-chain.uic.edu) at the University of Illinois at Chicago. The author or coauthor of over 150 articles, technical reports, and papers presented at professional meetings, he is the coauthor of the book the *External Environment of Business: Political Economic, Social and Regulatory*, Stipes Publishing Co., Champaign, IL, 1995, 2nd ed 1997. He has been Project Director or Project Manager of over 40 separate research and consulting projects.

In 2006, he served as President of the *Transportation Research Forum*, which is one of the oldest transportation professional organizations in the United States. He also was the co-founder and Co-General Editor of the *Journal of the Transportation Research Forum*, which publishes articles of interest to academics, policy makers, and practitioners. The journal has been ranked ninth in the field of US and international transportation-related journals by a panel of academic researchers.

Dr. Pagano was awarded a Fulbright Scholar grant to teach courses in international business, logistics, and supply chain management at Santa Maria La Antigua University in Panama City, Panama, in the spring of 2010. Additionally, he performed research in the area of analysis of maritime economic clusters for the Panama Canal Authority.

He teaches courses in supply chain and logistics, transportation economics and public policy, and international business. He has a PhD in Economics from the Pennsylvania State University. His website is www.uic.edu/~amp

Fazle Karim is an aspiring data scientist who is completing his PhD in the Mechanical and Industrial Engineering department at University of Illinois at Chicago. He received his BSIE in 2012 from the University of Illinois at Urbana Champaign. He is currently the lead data scientist at PROMINENT lab, the leading process mining research facility at the university. He has taught courses in Probability and Statistics in Engineering, Work Productivity Analysis, Quality Control and Reliability, and Safety Engineering. His research interest includes education data mining, health care data mining, and time series analysis.

Mr. William E. Stillman has been with GAINSystems, Inc. as a senior executive and one of its principal stockholders for just over 20 years. For ten years prior to forming a business partnership with the founder of GAINSystems, Mr. Stillman was the owner and CEO of Knowlex, Inc. Knowlex was a consulting firm specialized in helping scientists and engineers to commercialize their leading edge technologies as well as build successful commercial organizations around them. To the years leading up to his founding Knowlex, Mr. Stillman held various positions focused in International management and business development with Emerson Electric, GTE, and Apollo Computer.

Mr. Stillman holds an MBA from Washington University in St. Louis, MO and a BA from Principia College, in Elsah, IL. He is the author of "Off the Business Path: search for the creative process" by Ashcroft & Tate and has had articles published in CONNECT Magazine, The Christian Science Monitor, and Industry Week.

Mr. Stillman is currently working on a multilingual, executive case study book targeted at broadening the international business skills of senior executives and is a frequent on Supply Chain Profit Optimization.

Behzad Karimi is a Postdoc Scholar working at the Center for Urban Transportation Research (CUTR) at the University of South Florida (USF) and an Adjunct Faculty at the University of Tampa in Tampa, FL. He earned his PhD in Transportation Engineering from the University of Illinois at Chicago in 2015. His research areas of interest are travel behavior analysis, travel demand modeling, traffic safety, discrete choice analysis, and econometric modeling. His studies in recent years are Metropolitan Freight Transportation: Implementing Effective Strategies (NCHRP Project 08–106, 2016–17), MPO Staffing and Organizational Structure (FHWA/FTA, 2016–17), Florida's Comprehensive Motorcycle Safety Study (2016–17), Illinois High-Speed Rail Ridership Estimation (2012), Illinois Statewide Travel Demand Modeling (2015), Goods Movement Study in Illinois (2013), and Analysis of Seniors' Travel Behavior (2013). His paper in 2014 TRB's Data Contest received the Best Student Paper award.

J. Christopher Westland is a Professor in the Department of Information and Decision Sciences at the University of Illinois—Chicago. He has a BA in Statistics and an MBA in Accounting from Indiana University and received his PhD in Computers and Information Systems from the University of Michigan. Christopher has professional experience in the United States as a certified public accountant and as a consultant in technology law in the United States, Europe, Latin America, and Asia. He is the author of numerous academic papers and of seven books: *Global Electronic Commerce* (MIT Press 2000), *Global Innovation Management* (Palgrave Macmillan 2nd ed 2015; 2008), *Red Wired: China's Internet Revolution* (Marshall Cavendish 2010), *Structural Equation Modeling* (Springer 2015), *Financial Dynamics* (Wiley 2003), *Valuing Technology* (Wiley 2002), and *Financial Auditing with Information Technology* (Credere 2014). Christopher is the *Editor-in-Chief* of *Electronic Commerce Research* (Springer) and has served on editorial boards of several other information technology journals including Management Science, ISR, ECRA, IJEC, and others. He has served on the faculties at the University of Michigan, University of Southern California, Hong Kong University of Science and Technology, Tsinghua University, University of Science and Technology of China, Harbin Institute of Technology, and other academic institutions. In 2012, he received High-Level Foreign Expert status in China under the 1000-Talents Plan and he is currently Overseas Chair Professor at Beihang University. He has advised on patent, valuation, and technology strategy for numerous technology firms.

Mellissa Gyimah is a doctoral student studying Literacy Language and Culture at the University of Illinois at Chicago. Her research interests include race and reader response, textual lineages of Black students and teachers who instruct those students, and including Black texts within the literary canon and positioning theory. Being Black British she is concerned with the lack of variegated Black texts that represent Black immigrants, as well as African Americans within the high school literary canon and curricula. She has previously taught Secondary School English and P.E in Dover, UK, before completing her Master's in Writing and Publishing at DePaul University in 2013.

Zahra Pourabdollahi is a transportation consultant with RS&H since 2014. She received her PhD in transportation engineering from University of Illinois at Chicago in 2014 with her research focused on supply chain analysis and freight transportation modeling. Zahra has worked as the project manager for a significant multimodal freight transportation modeling project, developing an innovative supply chain model for the Arizona

Sun-corridor Megaregion. The project is part of the FHWA's Strategic Highway Research Program 2 (SHRP2-C20): Freight Demand Modeling and Data Improvement Strategic Plan for the Maricopa Association of Governments, Arizona. She has led the development of a tour-based freight model for the Tampa bay area to assess regional freight movements at a more detailed analysis scale. She is also involved with several transportation model and data projects for Florida Department of Transportation including Florida Statewide Tourism Trip Forecasting, Development of a Freight and Modal Data Plan, and Freight Performance Metrics Development.

Kouros Mohammadian is a Professor of Transportation Systems and Head of Civil and Materials Engineering Department at the University of Illinois at Chicago. He received his PhD from the University of Toronto in 2001. His research has covered various areas of transportation planning including travel behavior analysis, modeling of activity and travel patterns, travel surveys, computational analysis of transportation systems, agent-based microsimulation models, and freight and logistics modeling. Kouros has authored/coauthored over 280 scholarly publications in scientific journals, conference proceedings, book chapters, and reports. He is the co-editor-in-chief of the Journal of Transportation Letters and currently serves as Committee Chair of Transportation Research Board's "Traveler Behavior and Values" committee. He has received the Ryuichi Kitamura award, Fred Burggraf award, and Charley Wootan award from TRB, recognizing his contributions to transportation research.

Dr. Kazuya Kawamura's expertise includes freight transportation planning, economic impacts evaluation of transportation projects, transportation-land use interactions, and empirical evaluation of accessibility measures. He is a member of National Academies' Transportation Research Board committees on Freight Planning and Logistics. He has also served in Chicago Metropolitan Agency for Planning (CMAP) Freight Committee since its inception. He has been elected twice to the Governing Board of Association of Collegiate Schools of Planning. He holds a BS degree in Mechanical Engineering from the North Carolina State University, Raleigh and PhD and Master's in Civil Engineering from the University of California, Berkeley.

Siddhartha Varma Gadiraju is currently a Data Scientist at Capgemini. His work includes studying customer behavior patterns, and demand planning across industries backed by statistical analyses. Before joining Capgemini, Siddhartha held a Research Assistantship position at the Center for Supply Chain Management and Logistics at UIC, working with Professor Matthew Liotine and Professor Anthony Pagano. His primary area of research was in the innovative usage of technology in the North American supply chain space. He holds a BE degree in Electronics and Communications Engineering from Manipal University, and a Master's degree in Management Information Systems from the University of Illinois at Chicago.

Houshang Darabi is an Associate Professor of Industrial and Systems Engineering in the Department of Mechanical and Industrial Engineering at the University of Illinois at Chicago (UIC). He also holds an Associate Professor position in the Department of Computer Science at UIC. Darabi's main research interests include the application of data mining, process mining, and optimization in design and analysis of manufacturing, business, project management, and workflow management systems.

Darabi's research has been supported by several federal and private agencies such as the National Science Foundation, the National Institute of Standard and Technology, the Department of Energy, and Motorola. Darabi has published in different prestigious journals and conference proceedings such as IEEE Transactions on Robotics and Automation, IEEE Transactions on Automation Science and Engineering, IEEE Transactions on Systems, Man and Cybernetics, and Information Sciences. He has been a contributing author of two books in the area of Scalable Enterprise Systems and Reconfigurable Discrete Event Systems. He has extensively published on various automation and project management subjects including wireless sensory networks for location sensing, planning and management of projects with tasks requiring multi-mode resources, and workflow modeling and management. He is a senior member of the Institute of Industrial Engineers (IIE), and a senior member of the Institute of Electrical and Electronics Engineers (IEEE).

Index

OTHER TITLES IN OUR SUPPLY AND OPERATIONS MANAGEMENT COLLECTION

Joy M. Field, Boston College, Editor

- *Demand Forecasting for Managers* by Stephan Kolassa and Enno Siemsen
- *The Unified Theory of Profitability: 25 Ways to Accelerate Growth Through Operational Excellence* by Andrew Miller
- *Mapping Workflows and Managing Knowledge, Volume II: Dynamic Modeling of Formal and Tacit Knowledge to Improve Organizational Performance* by John L. Kmetz
- *RFID for the Supply Chain and Operations Professional, Second Edition* by Pamela Zelbst and Victor Sower
- *An Introduction to Lean Work Design: Fundamentals of Lean Operations, Volume I* by Lawrence D. Fredendall and Matthias Thürer
- *An Introduction to Lean Work Design: Standard Practices and Tools of Lean, Volume II* by Lawrence D. Fredendall and Matthias Thürer
- *Managing Commodity Price Risk: A Supply Chain Perspective, Second Edition* by George A. Zsidisin, Janet L. Hartley, Barbara Gaudenzi, and Lutz Kaufmann
- *Forecasting Fundamentals* by Nada Sanders
- *1 + 1 = 100: Achieving Breakthrough Results Through Partnerships* by Rick Pay

Announcing the Business Expert Press Digital Library

Concise e-books business students need for classroom and research

This book can also be purchased in an e-book collection by your library as

- a one-time purchase,
- that is owned forever,
- allows for simultaneous readers,
- has no restrictions on printing, and
- can be downloaded as PDFs from within the library community.

Our digital library collections are a great solution to beat the rising cost of textbooks. E-books can be loaded into their course management systems or onto students' e-book readers.
The **Business Expert Press** digital libraries are very affordable, with no obligation to buy in future years. For more information, please visit **www.businessexpertpress.com/librarians**. To set up a trial in the United States, please email **sales@businessexpertpress.com**.